José Silva, founder of the his investigations into parapsychology in 1944 in Laredo, Texas. A man with no formal education, he began to work with his own children to see if he could raise their IQ levels so that they would do better at school. After twenty-eight years of research and experimentation he developed the Silva Method and taught the first formal class in Amarillo, Texas, in 1966. The method has met with worldwide acclaim.

Also available from HarperCollins

THE SILVA METHOD
José Silva and Philip Miele

JOSÉ SILVA AND BURT GOLDMAN

The Silva Method of Mental Dynamics

The world's leading personal
development system

Unleash the power of your mind

HarperCollins*Publishers*

HarperCollins*Publishers*
77–85 Fulham Palace Road,
Hammersmith, London W6 8JB

This paperback edition 1996
1 3 5 7 9 8 6 4 2

Previously published in paperback by Grafton 1990
Reprinted twice

First published in the USA by Pocket Books
a division of Simon & Schuster Inc 1988

0 00 638781 0

Set in Times

Printed and bound in Great Britain by
Caledonian International Book Manufacturing Ltd, Glasgow

CONTENTS

Contents

INTRODUCTION

Since 1966, when the Silva Method of mind development was presented to the participants of that first class in Texas, the organization has grown remarkably. From its modest beginnings with one instructor and a handful of interested students, the Method has expanded to the present worldwide organization, with centers and offices in most major cities of the United States and branches in some seventy-five other countries, from Japan to Israel, Saudi Arabia to Ireland, China to Zimbabwe, Australia to Alaska. Millions of people from all professions, all walks of life, and all age groups, have listened to one of the 450 certified Silva instructors present the remarkable material of the Silva Method in any of eighteen languages.

What is it about this positive thinking philosophy that sets it apart from all others? Where does the phenomenal growth come from? And what is it that attracts all races, all religions, all classes, and all occupations of people to the Silva presentations?

The Silva Method threatens no one. Rather, Silva graduates report that they are more secure in their beliefs than ever before, since the method validates all the positive aspects of their lives. Appetites for life improve, relationships improve, health improves, and graduates become more self-aware and more understanding of others, tending to glide easily through life with the knowledge that they are not only responsible for their reality, but capable of controlling it.

This is the second major book on the Silva Method. The first, *The Silva Mind Control Method* by José Silva and Philip Miele (Grafton Books, 1980), explained the routine and sequence of the Silva basic lecture series classes, the fastest-growing self-help philosophy and problem-solving organization in the world. This follow-up book covers additional problem-solving techniques to help you understand how you are affected by outer influences in your life. You will find within these pages ideas and techniques on how to develop your own mind control to free you from the influence of outside agencies and to exercise greater control over your health, fortune, relationships, mental well-being, and virtually all other aspects of your life.

I myself can attest to the validity of the Silva method. When I first heard about José Silva, I was at a low point in my life because of a recent bankruptcy. Stressful and depressed, I went to one of the Silva classes and learned the methods and techniques. I was skeptical at first, but the results were magical. Six weeks after completing the short course, I was heading a new company and had more money, friends, and rewards than I would have dreamed of before my Silva training. Wanting to share the knowledge, I became a Silva instructor myself and then rose through the Silva ranks, eventually developing what was to become the Silva Mind Control Method of Mental Dynamics. Fine-tuned in close collaboration with José Silva and tested with thousands of graduates of my seminars, the concepts of Silva Mental Dynamics are now presented in this book.

To use Silva Mental Dynamics most effectively we recommend initially a cover-to-cover reading. Then, to find help with a particular problem, refer to the table of contents. Have a fight with your favorite aunt? See Chapter 21 on solving family problems. Going into business? See Chapters 23 through 26. Need a boost in confidence? See Chapter 10 on self-esteem. Tense and stressful? Chapters 1 and 6 deal with stress removal. For problems with a relationship, refer to Chapter 20. For a problem with flagging desire, read Chapter 19 (but watch out for this one—you don't want to overdo a good thing). Are fears a problem? See Chapter 7.

How many diets have you been on? You will probably find more answers to weight control in Chapter 16 than in any ten diet books you've read. And in Chapter 13, "Past Self, Future Self," you will find an effective method of overcoming problems that stem from past incidents. But the centerpiece of the book would have to be Chapter 2, "Switching Your Viewpoint to Love." Here you will find an explanation of the concept of the positive viewpoint presented so that you not only understand how it can help you immediately, but also how it can become an invaluable resource in your life.

Chapter 4, "The Seven Mighty Principles," will help you to understand the rules of life as they apply

9

to all things great and small. As these principles make clear, fear, courage, guilt, self-forgiveness, resentment, beauty, ugliness, hate, and love are all mental creations. Imagination, visualization, and all the inner constructs that correspond to the outer senses—these, too, are mental creations. Chapter 5, "Golden Images," deals with the creations of the mind and shows you how, through enhanced visualizations, to control those images to give you better control over your own mind.

Silva Mental Dynamics is based on the fact that perceptions stem from the use of the imagination. When that image-making faculty is directed in a negative manner, the world is dark and gloomy. When the imagery is directed in a positive manner, your world becomes bright, joyous, and cheerful. You can gain better control of your mind through the simple use of the Silva Mental Dynamic concepts and techniques. And you can direct that dynamic imagination to make a better and better life for yourself.

Burt Goldman
Palm Springs, California
1988

PART ONE

Silva Mental Dynamics Principles and Basic Techniques

Chapter 1

FIRST-STAGE MEDITATION

There is an underlying rhythm to all things that exist on this planet. Light has rhythm in the form of waves; sound too. Each color of the spectrum has its own rhythm. Your very heart pumps blood through your body in rhythmic beats. Similarly, scientists have discovered in recent decades, your brain activity produces waves that are measurable and that vary enormously according to your level of sleep or wakefulness, serenity or agitation, concentration or distraction, and even health or disease.

The rhythms of the brain are caused by all the excitements, desires, anxieties, stress, calmness—in short, all the various states of the human condition. Wouldn't it be remarkable if these rhythms could be controlled?

One of the most fundamental goals of Silva Mental Dynamics is to accomplish just this. Over the years that Silva techniques have been developed, refined, and practiced, hundreds of thousands of graduates have found how the ability to control their brain waves can literally change their lives. In this chapter we'll take a look at the way these brain waves function, their effect on one's total being, and some methods and benefits of controlling them.

Scientists have identified four basic types of brain waves—Beta, Alpha, Theta, and Delta—corresponding to four levels of brain activity. The frequency of each kind of brain wave, measured in cycles per second, is visible in graphs generated by an electro-encephalogram (EEG) hooked up to a person's skull.

At the lowest end of the scale of possible brain-wave activity is the production of one-half cycle per second; at the highest, eighty-five cycles per second. These figures are extremes for the deepest kind of sleep at the low point, and an epileptic seizure, when the brain is at its most excited state, at the high point. More common is four to forty cycles per second, representing deep sleep through intense excitement.

While each of the four areas overlaps with other adjacent areas, and every individual has a slightly different rate, the following generally holds true:

When you are in Delta, you produce brain waves of from one-half to four cycles per second (CPS). Delta is the zone of deep, unconscious sleep, a little-known area of total unawareness. When you are in Theta, you produce from five to seven CPS. Theta is the zone of deep, comfortable sleep, an area of complete and utter satisfaction. When in Alpha, you produce from eight to thirteen CPS. Alpha is the area of relaxing sleep and dreaming, sometimes also called REM (for rapid eye movement) because eyes flicker rapidly when you are dreaming. When in Beta, the outer, conscious, aware state, your brain produces waves of from fourteen to forty CPS. You are in Beta at this moment as you read.

The average person, at an average time, during an average day, is in the Beta area producing twenty-one CPS.* When excited by anger, resentment, jealousy, fear, nervousness, apprehension, or any stirring emotion, that rhythm increases and the brain activity rises to twenty-two, twenty-five, or more CPS. Poor health, excitability, poor learning ability, and weak concentration are due in part to an excessive degree of brain-wave activity.

The rhythm of good health, the rhythm of intelligence, the rhythm of concentration, the rhythm of ease—indeed, the rhythm of pure genius—lies in the area of brain-wave production that falls below nineteen cycles per second.

Let's look at the consequences of high brain-wave activity and contrast them with the benefits of lower rates.

Stress and anxiety are associated with a brain-wave production above twenty-one cycles per second. Almost everyone in the scientific and medical community agrees that stress is the underlying cause of many health problems. When the brain activity is above twenty-one CPS (the area of normal conscious activity), the mechanism that controls the envelope of outer immunity that every normal person has is depleted and the germ/virus community that is ever-present is

---

* Actually the brain produces all four segments simultaneously; the amplitude, consistency, and frequency of waves determine the predominant area of activity.

in some manner invited in. When the germ/virus enters the body, the inner immune system, functioning normally, destroys the invading forces of germ/virus and the individual remains healthy. When the immune system is depressed, however, the germ/virus multiplies and overwhelms the cells of the body, causing illness and disease.

Excessive brain-wave activity causes other problems besides ill health. When brain activity is above twenty-one cycles per second, concentration is ruined. The thoughts of the individual go through an upheaval and are barraged by a series of inconsequential matters. Thousands of constantly changing thoughts, seemingly out of control, keep the mind from concentrating on what is important.

In the high Beta area—forty cycles per second—it becomes increasingly difficult to concentrate on any one subject for long. You find yourself uneasy and cannot sit still. The mind flits from thought to thought like a bee buzzing from flower to flower; before the complete formation of one thought you're on to still another. It's difficult to remember things, and even your last thought vanishes like a dream that fades when you come to full wakefulness.

When excitement creates a high rate of brain-wave activity and increased brain energy, it builds forces that must be released. The mind dissipates this force through physical actions, and so the body is harassed and ordered about and you often find yourself doing things you later regret. The body, unable to utilize its natural consciousness and blocked by the demands of the psyche, grows weaker and less effective in fighting off the many problems presented to it.

If an excessive degree of brain-wave activity is at the root of so many problems, it would follow that the ability to control brain waves could help us to solve many of our problems. Indeed, keeping brain-wave activity to a lower rate has innumerable benefits. For one thing, it fosters the opposite of disease—or dis-ease.

When you are at ease, you are comfortable and relaxed. When you are at ease, your brain waves invariably show a slower rate, generally around nineteen cycles per second. A normal, healthy person producing less than twenty cycles per second of brain activity cannot be in a state of dis-ease; on the contrary, the person is at ease. When you are at ease, your defense mechanisms via the immune system are strong and you are usually able unconsciously to fight off the hoards of germ/virus families.

The midrange Alpha state—around ten cycles per second of brain-wave activity—is a restful, relaxed state. Consciously lowering your brain waves, you become focused and able to concentrate well. Achieving brain activity in the midrange Alpha area is useful for any activity requiring thought. Thoughts are more concrete here; you are better able to examine them and to become more aware of all their dimensions. This is the state of being in which the mind tends to separate from the body, and the bodily intelligence, with no interference from mind, adjusts and heals itself.

Psychosomatic problems are simply problems caused by the mind (psyche) getting in the way of the body (the soma). By relieving the body of the problems of the mind through the Alpha-generated separa-

17

tion of psyche and soma, physical problems often resolve themselves.

The natural and normal rate of brain activity when you are awake is the lower twenties and the high teens. The body's healing abilities at a lower rate of brain-wave production are seen in the way brain waves slow down naturally during an illness. When you are not feeling well you get lethargic and enervated. Rather than drive, walk, or even eat, you prefer to sit and doze, relaxed to a state in which the brain is producing fifteen cycles per second (Beta bordering on Alpha).

Elderly people often find themselves nodding off into a state of Alpha with increasing frequency. This is nothing to be feared but rather to be welcomed. Because the cells take longer to restore themselves and work harder to maintain the correct sodium–potassium balance, the mind temporarily relieves itself of the body so that the body can do its work of reconstruction in a natural manner. Alpha is the healing state of mind.

An easy way to achieve the Alpha state of ten cycles per second is through the meditative process. Meditation has a rhythm all its own, as does excitement, or anger, or for that matter any emotion that either stirs one up or calms one down. What meditation does is to slow down the brain waves and separate the mind from the body. This enables the mind to concentrate better, since it does not have to deal with the body's nervous or emotional manifestations, or its reactions to outer or inner stimuli.

As far as the body is concerned, without the mind to harass it, the bodily intelligence can do its work. Its main job is to keep the cells in an energized balance so that it can be stabilized in a healthy condition. The major health benefit of meditation, then, is keeping the mind from interfering with the body so both may do their respective jobs—the body healing itself when ill and remaining healthy when healthy.

The meditative technique we teach in the Silva Mind Control program of Mental Dynamics we call "going to level." By "level" we mean the ten-cycle-per-second, or Alpha level of brain-wave activity. Through much research and feedback we have determined that virtually everyone can achieve the level of ten cycles per second while maintaining awareness. By so doing, practitioners find themselves restored mentally and physically, and well rested for the daily routine of living.

Going to level is one of the basic building blocks of the Silva Method. In the chapters that follow, you will encounter many examples of advice and techniques that entail going to level. It is both a method rewarding in itself and an essential part of other problem-solving procedures. Going to level is the first stage of meditation, the initial step in consciously relaxing to the Alpha level of mind and a slower brain-wave frequency. In later chapters we will introduce deeper levels of meditation.

Here is the method for first-stage meditation, or going to your Alpha level.

Find yourself a comfortable place to sit; a couch or chair is fine. It is best if you can sit with your back straight and your spine supporting you. Close your eyes and take a slow, deep breath. As you slowly release your breath, mentally repeat and visualize the number three; say, "three, three, three." Then do the same with the number two, and then once again with the number one.

At this point you should be somewhat relaxed. If you are not, then start again and this time pay particular attention to the numbers. Visualize them clearly, make them brighter, and mentally paint them a color of your liking. That should focus your attention and relax you.

Take another deep breath and as you exhale, mentally say the word *relax,* very quietly and very slowly. Feel that each exhalation takes you deeper and relaxes you more.

Now start again, this time with the number ten, and count down, concluding with the number one. Feel yourself getting more relaxed with each descending number and you will be more relaxed.

How long you stay in your Alpha level, and what you do there, is up to you. You may simply relax there for a few minutes as stress dissolves; you may use it to open the channels of creativity or to ponder a sticky problem. As the following chapters suggest, you may use it to reinforce efforts to break unwanted habits, or to change yourself in ways you'd like—the possibilities are endless.

To come out of level, count from one to three and tell yourself that at the count of three your eyes will open, you will be wide-awake and alert, and you'll feel better than before.

And that is all there is to it.

As with any endeavor, you will improve as you practice. Improvement in this case means that ultimately you will simply close your eyes, take a deep breath, and be at level.

The "three-finger technique" may be used to activate the process and make it easier. This technique tells the mind, "Come to attention, something is about to take place." It strengthens your concentration so that you may ease into level. To use the three-finger technique, place the first three fingers of either hand together (the thumb, the forefinger, and the middle finger) and then think about what it is you wish to do, such as go to level. Then do it.

If you were to use the technique now, chances are it would not work for you because it has not yet been programmed; it isn't a trigger device yet. To make it a triggering mechanism, go to level and say to yourself, "All I have to do to accomplish things that I desire is to put the first three fingers of either hand together [now touch the first three fingers of either hand together]. This will take me to a deeper level of mind for successful programming." Do this every day for seven days and you will have programmed the three-finger technique. This is a wonderful resource to use during any anxious moments in your life, such as a stress-filled meeting, or boring moments, such as a long plane, train, or automobile trip, or even while sitting in a dentist's chair awaiting the drill. When you use the three-finger technique, be sure to visualize the desired end result of what you are programming when you bring your fingers together.

After practicing this method a few times you will find it quite easy to reach the Alpha level of mind. We recommend "going to level" at least once each day, just before bedtime if you have a sleep or health problem. If you are in good health and have no stress-related problems, practice going to level when you are more energetic than you are just before sleep; late afternoon before dinner is recommended.

If you have a health problem or are involved with any stressful situation, we recommend first-stage meditation three times a day. Five minutes each time is adequate, while ten minutes is better, and fifteen minutes is most beneficial.

Chapter 2

SWITCHING YOUR VIEWPOINT TO LOVE

One of the most used and least understood words in the English language has to be *love*. Over the centuries more atrocities, more mayhem and torture, more murders have been conceived and committed under the banner of love than in the name of any other concept. For love nations have attacked nations, families attacked families, all seeking to force their interpretation of the word on others, all thinking that they're right. Their "rightness," of course, made everyone else "wrong." Enforced and reinforced by the club, the ax, sword, arrow, and ultimately the gun and the bomb, love became justification for any act by the "right" toward the "wrong."

What really is this thing called love? The word *love* is truly an abstraction; having no meaning in itself, it is given meaning only when we attach something to it. The Greeks had many definitions for love: *agape*,

23

meaning spiritual love; *philos,* or brotherly love; *eros,* erotic or romantic love. But the definitions, too, are abstractions; they add little meaning to the word. For what does *philos* mean? It's just a word for one aspect of love. Eros is still another of the many facets of love. But what is *love?*

To arrive at an answer, let us rely on a useful and frequently invoked technique of Silva Mental Dynamics, polarization. The polarization technique is based on one of the fundamental principles of Silva Mental Dynamics—indeed, one of the basic principles of life (see Chapter 4, "The Seven Mighty Principles"). According to the principle of polarity, all things have an opposite and opposites are the same in nature, differing only by degree.

Applying that principle to help us understand the nature of love, let us imagine a gauge, a straight line, like a yardstick. On the left end of the line is the negative, on the extreme right is the positive, and in the center is the neutral area. Let us call love a viewpoint and examine the word from that perspective. On each end of our gauge we'll put the word *viewpoint.* On the positive end we now have a positive viewpoint, and on the opposite end a negative viewpoint. Above the positive viewpoint we'll put the word *love;* and above the negative viewpoint we'll put the word *hate.*

And so we are defining love as a positive viewpoint, and we find that according to the principle of polarity love and hate differ only by degree. Let's see if it fits.

Imagine a person who is the recipient of absolute love. Absolute love would be on the farthest right end of the scale where there are no negatives, only positives. So you can see this person only from a thoroughly positive viewpoint. You can find only the positives in this individual, no negatives. Whatever this person does, says, or acts like is seen in a positive light. You view everything about this person with all of the aspects of love.

Few people are the recipients of love to this degree, with perhaps two exceptions. There is an entire class of people who tend to receive love of this magnitude—babies. Most parents see only the positives in their babies, at least until the age of six months.

Sometimes young couples, too, respond to one another with the same extreme degree of love, seeing only the positive aspects of one another. Whatever the other person does or says is wonderful; whatever the other person looks like, he or she is seen as handsome or beautiful. Then time goes by and attitudes change. The viewpoint moves a bit toward the center of the scale, from the 100 percent mark to the 90 or 80, and the two begin to see what was always there but was overlooked in their starry-eyed, exclusively positive viewpoint. Love diminishes and may settle in to a nice comfortable level at which each person sees the negative aspects of the other but accepts them. They may try to change one another. They may try to avoid one another at certain times of the day, month, or year. But they have accepted one another and so they are content and happy with each other.

Love, then, is a positive viewpoint. Let's see how this definition is useful in your everyday life.

If you have a sink filled with dirty dishes, chances are it will fall on the hate part of the gauge, the negative end. You have a negative viewpoint toward dirty dishes. If dirty dishes are hateful, what is the best way to deal with them? The answer is to change your viewpoint. Do not think about washing dirty dishes any longer, for that image resides on the negative end of the scale, the hate end. Instead, go into your kitchen to sparkle it up, because a sparkling-clean kitchen is on the positive side of the gauge. Everyone loves a sparkling-clean kitchen. So switch your viewpoint, change from hate to love, and instead of going in to wash dirty dishes, go in and sparkle up the kitchen.

To use love as a force in your life, simply change your attitude or viewpoint toward the troublesome situation or event. Love is always a workable solution when it is seen as a positive viewpoint. What a difference it would have made over the centuries if instead of being told "Love thy neighbor," which is incomprehensible (especially if you were the lord of a castle and your neighbor was a goathered), we had been told "See thy neighbor from a positive point of view." That you can do. You can see the positive aspects and the good points of your neighbor. See the positive aspects not only of another person, but also of another country, another race, another profession. What a difference seeing the good in others makes in your attitude.

With the ability to switch your viewpoint, you have a wonderful tool at your disposal, a resource always available for your use. You can call upon this resource to change a gloomy, rain-laden day into one that fills you with wide-eyed wonder and excitement. You can transform a boring meal into one of the best you've ever eaten. Almost any negative factor in your life can be changed into a positive one.

Consider how many things there are that disturb you at present. The reason these things are troublesome to you is that you are seeing them with a negative viewpoint. Whether you realize it or not, you hate these things. Your hate could be mild, falling midrange on the negative side of the gauge rather than on the extreme end, but you can bet that it is on the negative side, for if it were not, the things would not bother you.

Two recent graduates of Silva Mental Dynamics, Harold and Grace M., were on a honeymoon in Europe, swimming in the Mediterranean, when someone ran off with their rented car and all of their possessions, including Grace's purse and Harold's wallet. Of course they were upset, but they asked themselves how in the world they could have a positive attitude about that. They talked the situation over with one another and decided that their honeymoon would become a grand adventure, with great opportunities to do things they never would have been able to do had they followed their original plan, structured for them by a Dallas travel agency.

They reported the theft to the local police. When the officer they spoke to heard their story he invited them home with him, treated them as family, and put them up until they could arrange to have relatives in Texas send additional funds. By the time the money arrived three days later, Harold and Grace had made so many friends that they decided to spend the remaining week of their honeymoon right there in the small village. If they were to do it again, they've said, they would not change a thing, including the theft of the auto.

When you go through something that seems to be negative in nature, remember there is always an opposite side. Change your attitude toward the situation and see it as a great challenge to be overcome, a test. When you do your best to get through it you will be the better for it, so long as you use your positive viewpoint. Be the best you can and life will be more pleasant and occasionally exhilarating.

To help you to switch your viewpoint, go to your level (as described in Chapter 1) and think about the matter that bothers you. Use the polarization technique to change your viewpoint from the negative to the positive. Visualize a horizontal gauge with degree marks on it. At the left end, the negative side, pile up all the negative things you can think about regarding this matter. On the right end, amass all the positives. Visualize a marker on the gauge at the negative end. Now mentally move the marker over to the positive side and at the same time concentrate on the positive aspects of the thing you wish to switch from the negative.

Going to level—and, when you're practiced enough, using the three-finger technique described in Chapter 1—should relieve you of some of the stress connected with the matter under consideration and allow your mind freedom and creativity to come up with many positive ways of perceiving.

One day in one of our seminars, a furniture retailer who owned a few large stores told the class about something that was a source of constant irritation in his work: the many complaints that he would get. He sold fine, expensive furniture and dealt primarily with decorators, who, wishing to please their clients, assured them of absolute perfection. The furniture dealer could not produce perfection; occasionally a minor blemish would appear on one of his couches or chairs, or a dye lot would differ slightly from the original sample.

The complaints were handled by three people who worked at a switchboard near his office in the main store. Although it was only one part of their job, people who were on that desk continually quit. No one liked complaints. His employees didn't want to be targets for the abuse they received.

So our businessman, tired of constantly hiring new people for that job, went to his meditative level and thought about the problem. He thought about this business of love being a positive viewpoint, and he thought about the dirty dishes and the sparkling-clean kitchen. How could he take the dirty dishes of the complaints, he wondered, and turn them into a sparkling-clean kitchen?

He reported that he pondered the matter for a good many days. He knew that somehow there had to be a way in which he could switch his viewpoint and that of his complaint department personnel. One morning when he woke up it came to him. He snapped his fingers, and for the first time in many a month couldn't wait to get into his office. He called a sign maker and had a large sign painted. At the top of the sign appeared these words: MANIAC OF THE MONTH CLUB. The board was separated into three columns, each headed with the name of one of the three people who were currently working the complaint desk. Whenever a complaint came in, he told each one, give it a rating from one to ten. A one was the mildest complaint, while a ten was irresolvable. He told them that if the complaint could be settled by them over the phone, it was a one; if a man had to be sent to the job to solve the problem it was a three; if he himself was the only one who could solve it, it was a five; and if it seemed to be unsolvable, it was to receive a ten. He expected most of the complaints to be threes and fives. Those working the complaints had to be honest about their ratings, for there would be a reward for whoever got the worst complaints each month.

There was a lot of excitement in his store the day he explained all this to the three working the board. Every time a complaint came in, whoever was on the phone would nod and smile to the others—a far cry from the earlier grimness about the ordeal. His complaint taker would hang up the phone, run to the new board, and write down the rating—usually 1, 3, or 5. The next day, all three of them were in the store right on the dot of nine, fired up and waiting for the phones to start ringing with complaints. The inevitable problems would begin, and every now and then somebody would yell out, "Oh boy, you ought to hear this one." And on the board would go a big number 5. Soon the complaint desk became one of the most popular departments in the store. The businessman gave a reward of $100 at the end of each month for the employee who had accumulated the most points. Instead of threatening to quit, people began asking for a turn at complaints.

He had done it. He had changed a hateful job into one that everyone wanted simply by switching viewpoints: the worse the complaint, the better they now liked it. They no longer washed dirty dishes. What they were now doing was sparkling up their kitchens.

What is it in your life that you can sparkle up? Use this concept of love to change bothersome aspects of your life. Use this concept of love by switching from a negative viewpoint to a positive one. Especially in conjunction with Chapter 3, "Five Rules of Happiness," the ideas and techniques here offer you the basis for changing your whole life.

An event that took place after one of our seminars is a good illustration of the dynamic use of this principle. One day Roger G. phoned one of our instructors to report how effectively he had used the Silva Method to solve a problem involving his thirteen-year-old son, Shawn. Shawn wanted to earn some extra money and had his father drop him off in a nearby neighborhood with a basket of stencils, paint, and brushes. Shawn was going to paint numbers on the curbs in front of houses. The numbers would make it easier to identify the address. Shawn would sell his service for one dollar.

Roger, a salesman, was easing his son into the profession. Even if Shawn did not take to sales, at least he would have a better idea of what his father did, and that was Roger's primary interest. He felt that this was an easy sell and that his son might even make a few dollars at it. Shawn, who had never tried anything like it before, was excited and could hardly wait to begin.

Roger dropped Shawn off in a residential neighborhood and promised to return within two hours. An hour and a half later Roger pulled up to a curb where Shawn sat, his chin resting on his fist, with a dejected look on his face that brightened when he realized he was being picked up.

Dropping his basket on the floor of the car with a bang, he sat heavily on the back seat and sighed. "Boy, Dad, I don't know how you do it. That was the worst experience I've ever had in my whole life. I don't ever want to do that again."

Needless to say, his father was disappointed. He asked, "What happened, Shawn? Didn't anybody buy the service?"

"Oh yeah," replied his son, "a few people paid me a dollar to paint their numbers on the curb. It was the ones who slammed the door in my face that bothered me." And shaking his head he asked again, "How do you do it, Dad? How can you take that?"

"Take what? What are you talking about, son?" Roger asked.

"You know what I mean. People are so nasty. They cursed me, and threw me out of their houses. Some of them yelled at me. I didn't realize that people were so mean."

On questioning, it turned out that none of these things were really happening, although Shawn thought that they were. He had faced, for the first time in his life, the bane of the sales profession, rejection. At age thirteen he had never gotten so much of it in so short a period of time. Everyone, it seemed to him, rejected him—which to him meant that they didn't like him. It was too much; he couldn't handle it and would never expose himself to that experience again. "Well, did you sell any?" his father asked.

Shawn reached into his pocket and pulled out a crinkled dollar bill, and then a few more until he had

32

accumulated a small pile. His father's eyes opened a bit wider as he asked, "How much is there?"

Shawn counted and said, "Six dollars."

"Six dollars!" his father exclaimed. "But Shawn, that's terrific. You were only out for an hour and a half and you made six dollars. I think that's pretty good."

"No, it's not" was the reply. "I'm not going out there again, I hate it. I'd rather do anything than knock on doors again."

"How many people did you call on, Shawn?" his father asked.

"About a thousand."

His father shook his head seriously and said, "Shawn, you must be mistaken. You weren't out long enough to call on a thousand people."

"Well then, maybe fifty or sixty," he said after thinking about it for a moment.

"You know, Shawn," his father began, "if you called on sixty people and made six dollars that means you sold ten percent of them. That's a pretty good average." Shawn's features took on the look of total misery at that statement, and his father chuckled and quickly added, "It's okay, son, I'm not going to make you go out anymore." He shrugged and continued, "At least you know what it's all about now."

Roger reported that here was a good test case for the changing of a viewpoint for him to use. Shawn had a negative attitude toward selling that Roger was going to turn around so that his son would have a positive attitude and taste success.

Shawn was a recent graduate of the Silva children's class, and he had seen some spectacular events take place at the seminar for youngsters. He had been a participant in many of them, so what Roger said did not seem at all strange to him.

"Shawn," his father asked, "how would you like me to put a spell on you so that every time you knock on a door, the person answering will pay you a dollar to paint the house number on the curb?"

"Every one of them?" Shawn asked.

"Every one," Roger answered.

"Sure."

For it wasn't the selling he feared; it was the rejection. If it could be guaranteed that he would make a sale in every house, then he did not have to fear rejection. The most timid salesperson in the world would have the courage of a tiger if every call were guaranteed to result in a sale.

Thirteen-year-old Shawn G. stood outside the car while Roger put the spell on him. Pointing his index finger at Shawn's chest Roger quickly moved his arm to describe a five-pointed star in the air, finishing with a dot in the center of the star as a nice flourish, while Shawn stood with his chest out as though catching the symbol.

"That's it," Roger said.

"Now let me get this straight," Shawn said. "Every person I call on will buy?"

"Yes," Roger said. Shawn grabbed his basket of paint and started off. "Wait a minute," his father cried. Back Shawn came to hear what more he had to say. "You know, Shawn," Roger said, "on second thought it wouldn't be fair if you were to sell every one. Have you ever heard me speak about paying your dues?"

He had, and he understood that if it was too easy it might hurt his growth and that he had to take a few knocks just so he could experience what people with less resources had to experience.

"Well," Roger said, "this is the way the spell is going to work. You call on fifty people. The first forty-five will all say no. The next five will all buy. Can you handle that?"

"Sure," Shawn said, "but I'm going to get past them as quickly as I can."

"That's all right," Roger replied, "so long as you knock on fifty doors. But, Shawn," he continued, "I really don't have complete control over this spell. Some of the five might slip into the forty-five, so here." Handing him a piece of paper and a pencil he said, "Every time you speak to a person, make a mark here so that you can keep score, and if one of the five slips in and you accidentally sell them, circle the mark. When you get to number forty-five, if two people have bought, then only the next three will buy."

Off he went, skeptical but game. Roger left to have a cup of coffee and returned about an hour later. Shawn was walking briskly down the street, paint all over his pants. When he noticed his father he waved and Roger pulled over.

"Wow!" he exclaimed. "That spell really works, I'm selling like crazy. Dad, how about leaving me here, I'll take a bus back. I don't want to quit just yet, there's plenty of paint left in the can and I have the rest of the next block to work."

Roger told the story just as it happened. The method worked; his son's viewpoint changed. The first time he knocked on doors, every door was a potential rejection. Shawn hated that. He hated the feeling that his finger on the doorbell or his knuckles knocking on the door would bring a person who rejected him. He couldn't deal with that for very long.

But after the so-called spell, which you might liken to the placebo effect because Shawn believed that the spell was going to influence the people he called on, everything changed. Forty-five people were going to say no. That's not rejection. That's just a job to do, to get past those forty-five as quickly as possible so he could get to the five who were going to buy.

As long as he believed that, he could be a tiger. He not only didn't care any longer if they slammed the door in his face, he welcomed it, and the quicker they did it the better. He would scratch off one more on his way to number forty-five.

Of course what was happening was that his enthusiasm and courage showed through and the percentage of his sales increased dramatically. More and more of the magic five slipped through. By the time he reached the forty-fifth person he was so involved with the spell that counting was no longer necessary and he began to greet a resounding "no" with an "Oh boy, another one out of the way."

His viewpoint had been changed. Instead of seeing the door from a negative viewpoint (hate), he began to see it from a positive viewpoint (love), and that helped him to achieve his goal.

Incidentally, there is a postscript to the story. Roger had inadvertently created a monster. Shawn's introduction to sales took place during summer vacation, and it wasn't long before he was making $200 a week and had two of his friends working for him. It took all of his father's power of persuasion to get him back into school at vacation's end.

* * *

How can this be applied in your own life? Consider something that you are now doing but not enjoying. If you must do it, for whatever reason, then use the tools you have now learned. Think about the positive aspects of the thing that you are doing. There must be some positive aspect to it—otherwise, why are you doing it? When you have determined its positive aspects, go again to your Alpha level and focus in on them. Visualize what there is to enjoy. Imagine yourself enjoying it. And then enjoy it.

Make the big switch from hate to love, and you will enjoy life more. Then the affirmation "Every day, in every way, I'm getting better and better" will truly take root and your life will indeed get better and better.

Chapter 3

FIVE RULES OF HAPPINESS

It almost seems silly to define happiness. You know when you're happy, and certainly no one has to tell you when you're sad. But what is it that makes a person happy? You might initially think of all kinds of experiences. Music makes me happy, ice cream makes me happy, or he or she makes me happy. Or housework makes me unhappy, Aunt Mabel makes me sad, and so on.

It is important to realize, however, that what makes you happy might make another person sad. What makes another person happy may make you sad. A fourteen-foot motorboat will make some people ecstatic. The high point of their lives could be the attainment of that boat. But to someone who covets a thirty-foot yacht, that fourteen-foot runabout could be a source of disappointment, of unhappiness. And those who don't care at all for boats would be neutral about the whole thing. One person you present with a cute little puppy is delighted; another can't stand dogs and now has to get rid of the poor animal.

And so we cannot use possessions as a criterion for happiness. For things are subjective, things are always relative to the individual and the individual's viewpoint. Instead, we will use a philosophy.

This philosophy is about enjoying things you like, avoiding or changing things you do not like, and accepting what you cannot avoid or change by the skillful use of your viewpoint. The use of this philosophy, as embodied in five rules, will allow you to test many problem areas in your life and find solutions.

Here, then, are the five rules of happiness.

Rule number one: If you like a thing, enjoy it. Now that seems outrageously simple. At first you might say, "That's ridiculous, of course if I like something I'm going to enjoy it." But when you stop to think about that statement you'll probably agree that there are many things in life that we like but don't enjoy. The reasons we don't enjoy things we like are (a) guilt, and (b) fear. You will not enjoy something you like if you feel guilty after having done the thing, or if you are fearful of the consequences of doing it.

Rule number two: If you don't like a thing, avoid it. The second rule seems simple enough, but reflect for a moment on how many people are involved with things they do not like—a job, a person, a vehicle, a type of food, any one of a thousand things—and for some reason they don't avoid those things. "Well, I can't avoid it. I have to work there because I need the money." Or, "I have to be involved with this person for many valid reasons." How many justifications can you think of for not avoiding the things you do not like to do?

Rule number three: If you don't like a thing and you cannot avoid it, change it. Here again, the answer is simple: change it. But just as in avoidance we rationalize that we need something about it—the money, the time, the security—something is holding you to that particular thing if you don't like it, cannot avoid it, won't change it, but are still involved with it.

Rule number four: If you don't like a thing, cannot avoid it, and cannot or will not change it, accept it. Accept it—now there is a catch. How can you accept something you don't like? You may have a favorite aunt whom you love very much but whose upper plate drops on her lower plate with a clack every time she says a word with an *s* in it; and your name is Shirley. You detest that and yet you love the woman, so you cannot avoid her; and you've tried changing her by offering to buy her another set of dentures but she likes the one that she has for whatever reason and so you cannot change her either.

How in the world do you accept something like that? How do you accept a situation that you're not happy with? How do you accept a person that you're not happy with? Well, you really don't have to accept anything; you can, of course, be unhappy. If you don't like it, won't change it, cannot avoid it, and *will not accept it*, I guarantee that you will be unhappy. There are, however, five rules to the secret of happiness, and within the fifth lies the key.

Rule number five: You accept a thing by changing your viewpoint of it. You are your viewpoint. Everything is relative to the person experiencing it. There are no absolutes—nothing is good, nothing bad, except as it relates to you. Nor is life good or bad. Life simply is. You can change those things you wish by changing your viewpoint about them. How to change your viewpoint is discussed in Chapter 2, "Switching Your Viewpoint to Love." For now, a brief example should serve to illustrate the fifth rule of happiness.

During a lunch break at a Silva Mental Dynamics seminar, one of our participants, George S., decided to drive to a nearby restaurant. He walked out to the parking lot and saw that his car had a fresh dent in the right front fender. Somebody had backed into his automobile, dented the fender, and driven off. He didn't like it; he couldn't avoid it, it was there; and he couldn't change it. That left him with the choice of being either happy or unhappy about the experience. George chose happy. He chose to change his viewpoint. When he looked at the fender, he no longer saw a dent that would cost him lots of money and time to have repaired but instead saw it as a stimulus to achieve something positive. Trying to imagine a positive outcome of the dent, he determined to earn triple the amount that it would cost to repair the fender. The body and fender shop quoted a price of $250 to fix the fender, and he set a goal for himself of earning $750. And he did.

George had totally polarized his relationship to the dented fender. *He didn't like it, he couldn't avoid it, and he couldn't change it, but he could change his viewpoint of it.* When he looked at the fender he saw $750. He set a goal for himself to earn the money and so he did. He earned his $750, paid the $250 repair bill, and actually came out $500 ahead and with happy thrown in for good measure. He stayed happy even though he had an experience that would cause most people a great deal of anguish.

* * *

PRINCIPLES AND BASIC TECHNIQUES

After going to your meditative level and using these five rules, you'll find yourself being reacquainted with happiness. You'll realize why people are unhappy. Eventually it will become automatic, and you'll find happiness a predominant state of mind. Once you realize the ease of acquiring this emotion, you develop an entirely new scale of highs and lows.

Unremitting happiness, of course, is not a possible—or desirable—state. According to the principle of rhythm (see Chapter 4), there is always an inflow and outflow, an ebb tide and a flood tide. You'll always have highs and lows—there's no way to avoid that. However, your highs will be higher and your lows will be higher. And you'll find that what is a depressive state for you might be a moderately happy state for someone unaware of the Five Rules of Happiness.

Chapter 4

THE SEVEN MIGHTY PRINCIPLES

In Greek mythology he was identified as the messenger of the gods. Hermes Trismegistus, "three times great," is what the ancient Greeks called him. The Romans called him Mercury and pictured him with winged shoes and hat. Known as the father of science, eloquence, and cunning, Hermes was also the protector of boundary lines and commerce. He founded alchemy, which ultimately became the art of chemistry and medicine; astrology, which formed the basis of astronomy, and mathematics, philosophy, and virtually all of the modern sciences.

Hermes, reputed to be a contemporary of Abraham, developed much of what was to become the basis for all esoteric teachings. The "Hermetic principles" can be found in both the most ancient of the Indian teachings and in the scrolls of the ancient Egyptians, for wise men came from all lands to sit at the feet of the Master Adept. For more than a millennium his teachings have remained hidden, known to very few.

They became enshrouded in the mysteries of occultism when the dark ages settled over Europe and the land was rife with the guardians of the faith who would torture and kill all who dared investigate the "dark secrets."

Today much is written about the knowledge of Hermes and especially about the Seven Principles he posited, which form the keystone of all knowledge. Their rediscovery by scholars unearthing ancient manuscripts in the quest for the age-old wisdom has brought them widespread interest in recent years. We offer the principles to you in the hope they will serve to help you too to grow and to mature.

To gain the most benefit from the Seven Principles you should go to level and meditate on each one. As you do, your level of awareness will rise and you will be a step further on the road to enlightenment. Do not expect understanding to come as a flash of inspirational lightning; rather, it comes gradually as each principle is thought about, digested, and used.

The Seven Principles influence all things and are immutable. They cannot be changed, modified, or destroyed. Their function can be likened to the rules of the road. Because they are universal rules, they govern all things, from the smallest particle to the expanding universe itself. An understanding of these rules gives you a step up on the game of life. These principles are the rules of life.

The first of the mighty principles is that of *mentalism*. The principle of mentalism states: *The universe is a mental creation of God.* Now immediately we run into the great problem with this principle: it is generally misunderstood by most people. Does it mean that we are a dream of some infinite entity so far removed from us that we may never hope to gather a glimmer of understanding of the nature of God, and therefore ourselves? Are we powerless robots of some omnipotent lab scientist? Not so. Just as the character in a novel is a creation of the novelist and is, therefore, an aspect of the novelist, so are we and everything else in the universe a part of the Creator. We are aspects of the totality of Creation. As we are relative to God, so is our universe relative to us. Your world is very real and very much yours. But it may not be my world at all, for in the relative sense, my world is a mental creation of my mind, just as yours is of your mind.

This principle can lead to a better understanding of our own minds and how they work. Mental power, or as we call it, mind control, works because the universe is mental. All things are seen from the relative position of your mind and what you think you see. You may think you see a tree, whereas a squirrel thinks it sees a home. Your friend may think that a Picasso is a fine wall decoration and you may think that it's a great investment. You may see a situation as a problem and your spouse may think that it's a challenge and see the solution. Of course, everyone is correct because what you think you see, you do see. The Silva Method is based on the fact that the mind can control forces and events outside oneself. This is a fact only because the world we see is our own mental creation; that being so, if we created it, we can recreate it. Silva graduates use their minds to change and to control their world.

* * *

The second principle to meditate upon is the principle of *correspondence*, which states, *"As above, so below; as below, so above."*

As it is on the physical plane, so it is on the mental; as it is on the mental plane, so it is on the spiritual. Just as your brain waves may be in high Beta at forty cycles per second, so is your emotional experience one of extreme agitation. Just as the universe is a mental creation of God, so is your personal world a mental creation of your own.

Understanding this principle will help you to unlock many emotions both positive and negative. It also helps you to tackle any problem area that has a range of manifestations: by dealing first with the easier, less intense manifestation of your problem, you will be solving, in some measure, the same problem in its most extreme form (see Chapter 17, "Assertiveness and Unvictimization"). There are many ways the principle of correspondence applies to Silva Mental Dynamics, as you'll see in the following pages, as well as in your everyday life.

The third principle is that of *vibration,* which states: *All things are in constant and never-ending motion. A change in the vibration causes a change in the manifestation.* Health has a vibration. Illness has a vibration. Success has a vibration and failure has a vibration. By changing the vibration you change the manifestation. Water at a high vibration is steam. Water at a low vibration is ice. But water, ice, and steam are the same, differing only in the vibration, which causes the change in the manifestation.

The first note on the musical scale is A. On the piano, the A just above middle C vibrates at the rate of 880 cycles per second (if the piano is properly tuned). Therefore 880 CPS represents A. Every single time. If you had a guitar and loosened the A string so that it now vibrated at 870 cycles per second, the sound would be a bit off. A fine ear would say that it's flat. The A, you might say, would have a slight cold; it would be a bit ill.

Loosen the A string even more so that it vibrates at 860 CPS and it would be way off. Even if you do not know an A from a G, you would know that it doesn't sound right. The A is now very ill; it has pneumonia. Loosen the string more and the A is no longer recognizable; it died. But not to worry, it's easy to resurrect an A. You simply tighten up the string.

As above, so below; as below, so above. As it is with a guitar string, so it is with your body. For when you are ill, what is at the root of the problem is that your vibrations are off. Adjust the vibrations to the proper level and a healing takes place.

The fourth great principle is the principle of *polarity*, which states: *All things are dual. Everything has its pair of opposites and these opposites are identical in nature, differing only in degree.* Tall and short are the same. There are tall little people and there are short basketball players. There is no such thing as tall or short, only as it is relative to you. Hot and cold are the same, as we've shown in the principle of vibration. We use polarity to swing from dislike to like, from fear to faith, from hate to love. It helps us to go from guilt to self-forgiveness, and from anger to tolerance.

We use this principle frequently to shed light on the meaning of words like love, fear, and anger, defining the word by examining its opposite. Take the word *fear,* for instance. What is it? A negative, certainly. But a negative what? If you were to draw a scale of polarity with a negative on one end and a positive on the other, you would place fear on the negative side. After some thought you would conclude that it was an expectation. Keeping within the nature of the word, you would place expectation on the negative end and also on the positive side. Fear is a *negative* expectation; you are expecting something bad to happen. Faith is a *positive* expectation; you are expecting something good to happen. Therefore fear and faith are the same, differing only by the degree of positiveness or the degree of negativeness. Change the degree and you change the emotion.

The fifth principle is the principle of *rhythm,* which states: *All things have their tides, an ebb tide and a flood tide.* All things rise and fall. There is a rhythmic cycle of birth, growth, deterioration, and demise in all things. There are cycles and rhythmic functions that affect us constantly, every moment of the day. When you wake up, your day is born. You begin the cycle of the day. When you eat breakfast, you start a cycle that concludes when you finish breakfast. Your day dies when you go to sleep, at which time your nighttime cycle is born. Your dreams are a cycle. Everything you do during the day is a cycle. You never know where you are on that cycle except in retrospect.

When things are taken at the flood, they are more likely to be successful. We all have a high point in our cycles, and a low point. This includes the sleep cycle, health cycle, energy cycle, success cycle, luck cycle, and so on. Each cycle has a different time period to run. The cycle of the moon, like the menstrual cycle, runs twenty-eight days; the sleep cycle runs ninety minutes. Most of the other cycles, however, remain hidden from us. If you were to chart your life with respect to colds, energy, luck, romance, enthusiasm, and lethargy, you would find a rhythm just as you will in all things. To discover more about your life cycles, go to level and use the three-finger technique. Tell yourself that at level you wish to examine and become more aware of whatever cycle of activity you want to know more about. Gambling during the high point of your luck period would bring you good luck. Shopping for a house at the height of your success period will find you the best house for you. Salespeople will find there are certain periods of the month when they can do no wrong. And so it goes.

The sixth mighty principle is the principle of *cause and effect,* which states: *Every cause has its effect and every effect its cause.* All things happen according to law. Accident and coincidence are the result of unrecognized cause.

A brief story will illustrate this principle. One day a leaf fell in a California forest. It landed on the forest floor, and a fat green caterpillar that was inching along had to make a sharp turn to avoid it. The caterpillar came to a log and crawled up the side. Just as it reached the top of the log, a man came by and sat down, squishing the caterpillar. The man jumped up and felt the goo on the seat of his pants. On returning home, he changed clothes and took the pants to the local cleaners. While there he met a young woman and they began a conversation, which continued at a nearby coffee shop. They began to date, fell in love, married, and had a child. Their son, being very clever, did well in school, became an attorney, and then went into politics, rising in his party.

And so, because a leaf fell in the forest one day, Richard Nixon became the thirty-seventh president of the United States. Cause and effect.

The seventh principle is the principle of *gender*, which states: *All things have a masculine and feminine aspect.* Gender manifests on the physical plane, on the mental plane, and on the spiritual plane. The masculine force is the outgoing, the positive, the instigative. The feminine force is the incoming, the receptive, the negative, the creative. This has nothing whatever to do with the male and female sexes, although they are manifestations of the principle of gender on physical planes. A dynamic speaker, for instance, is producing a masculine force while speaking, whether the speaker is male or female. This principle is treated more in depth in Chapter 24, "Communication."

These seven principles are immutable laws of nature. They cannot be changed or destroyed. However, law can be used against law, the higher against the lower, the lower against the higher. A log being swept down a stream is at the mercy of the current. A person swimming in the stream can use the principles of cause and effect, action and reaction to gain the shore. It is not necessary to have an understanding of these laws to be able to reach the shore; you simply swim there. However, an understanding will enable you to think at the shore what could be done if you were to fall into the river. Carrying the metaphor forward, we might say that the universe is a river, the planet is a river, the mind is a river.

These principles are for you to meditate on, to understand, and to work with so that they can help you in all aspects of your life. Their usefulness will unfold as you continue to grow and to evolve. Many of the manifestations of the principles are obvious, and some are more difficult to see, but every one of them underlies all the chapters of this book—and, you'll discover, of all others as well.

When we speak of programming by sending out a mental message via the Center Stage concept (Chapter 12), see how the forces of gender are at work. Or when using assertiveness to unvictimize yourself, see the correspondence principle at work. See how the principle of vibration works with respect to illness and health. Have a better understanding of cause and effect and create new cause by setting goals, as described in Chapter 23, "Setting and Achieving Goals." Use polarity to change from the negative to the positive, from fear to faith, from hate to love.

Chapter 5

GOLDEN IMAGES

People who enjoy washing dishes go into the kitchen to clean up with a vision of a sinktop clean and neat, cupboards filled with fresh, dry, clean dishes, the stove sparkling, and the utensils all put away. This is the subconscious mental image created by the person who loves doing dishes. This person does not visualize a sink full of dirty dishes, but rather a sparkling-clean kitchen.

The one who dislikes doing dishes has a visual image of dirty dishes, a stain-filled sink, a messy stove, and grease and dirt all over the place. It's no wonder this one hates to do dishes.

Our mental imagery makes us the people we are in every aspect of our lives. Our world, our realities exist in our minds, and our mental images can make our world a paradise or a hell. Recognition of this fact has given rise to one of the most versatile and powerful techniques in the Silva Mental Dynamics repertoire, that of the Golden Image.

The concept of the Golden Image is based on the power of your mental images to affect your behavior. The concept was first introduced in the Silva Basic Lecture Series in 1966. The technique involves "blue framing" things that you wish to diminish and rid yourself of and "white framing" things that you want to enhance and attract in order to give you better control over your life. When something bothers you, or causes you to be fearful, guilty, or resentful, you always create an image of that thing as well as an image of its opposite. If you fear something you bring in an image of the opposite of that fear. If you feared heights, for instance, you could imagine that you were an eagle soaring joyously over the frightening area. If you feared worms, you might picture them industriously at work aerating and fertilizing the ground so that giant plants can grow and feed hungry children. Fearing public speaking, you could visualize yourself addressing a rapt audience and being congratulated after a successful talk.

If you have a habit you want to break, determine what you would like to substitute for that habit; this is the experience and picture you will use. Say that you wish to stop smoking and the habit you would like to substitute for the cigarette smoking is sipping a bit of water, so that every time you have a desire to smoke, you will now want to sip a bit of water.

The basic difference between visualization and daydreaming is that the former is consciously creative and the latter is recreational.

Here, then, is the Golden Image technique.

Sit comfortably and go to level. Now visualize yourself smoking. Put a blue frame around the scene. Make the scene large, colorful, and dynamic. Give it movement. Bring in as many senses as you are able. Get a sense of the odor of cigarettes, of touch, of taste. Make the scene three-dimensional.

Next, create a white-framed image of the thing you wish to substitute for the habit. Make the white-framed image quite small, about a tenth of the size of the blue-framed image. Imagine the white-framed image at the lower left-hand corner of the large blue-framed image. In the white-framed image put a picture of you sipping from a glass of water. Leave the scene fuzzy, black-and-white, flat, and small.

When you have both images set, count to yourself, "One, two, three." At the count of three, say "Switch" and switch images. Now the blue-framed image with the picture of you smoking is the smaller and the white-framed image with the picture of you sipping a glass of water is the larger. Put the smaller, blue-framed image at the lower right side of the now larger, white-framed image. The right side represents the past; the left side represents the future.

The white-framed image always represents what you want to enhance. The blue-framed image always represents what you want to diminish.

The next step is to make the scene golden. You enhance the scene in the white-framed image. You diminish the scene in the blue-framed image. In the white frame you see yourself sipping water. Make the scene larger, three-dimensional; give it more depth, more color, more vividness. Bring in other senses such as taste and touch.

Do the opposite with the blue-framed image. Make it smaller. Make it fuzzy, out of focus, black-and-white. Make it still smaller, flat and one-dimensional.

You see yourself smoking in the blue frame but the scene is getting so small that soon it is the size of a bean. In the meantime the white-framed image is growing larger, brighter, and sharper. The blue-framed image disappears from the scene.

That is how you can deal with a fear or a habit. But there is much more to it than that. To illustrate, we'll tell you the story of Stanley E. and see how you can use it for motivating yourself.

Stanley E., a Silva Mental Dynamics student, had a problem. He procrastinated so often that he seldom got anything accomplished. He attended the Silva Mental Dynamics class to see whether there was something there to help him overcome his problem. Stanley was about five feet eight inches tall, weighed some 240 pounds, smoked a bit too much, drank a bit too much, and after work would sit in front of his TV until it was time for sleep.

He enjoyed fishing but kept putting off going; he always seemed too tired, and the TV was convenient and more comfortable. He enjoyed movies, but that meant leaving the house and so he seldom attended one. He wanted to go to the Caribbean for a vacation but that would require so much effort that it was out of the question.

In his bedroom was a corner that he used as an office. It was stuffed with papers, pencils, bric-a-brac, paper clips, and trash of all sorts that he was going to straighten out one day. But the call of the TV was overwhelming, and try as he might, it seemed that all he had to do was to begin a cleanup campaign and he would invariably wind up sipping a beer while watching TV.

Could Silva Mental Dynamics help him to overcome the devilment of procrastination? he wondered. It was worth a try and so he attended.

"How can I wipe procrastination out of my life?" he asked the instructor on the first day.

"Why do you want to do that?" he was asked in response.

Stanley looked bewildered. Everyone would want to do that, he thought, but he said, "Because procrastination is ruining my life. It controls me. It uses me. It won't let me do the things I enjoy."

The instructor laughed and nodded; that was an old story. But his reply was "Procrastination can be a valuable resource in your life, a great tool. Why not control it? Why not use it?"

He really looked befuddled now. Scratching his head, he said, "A resource? But it's such a negative thing. How can I possibly put it to any constructive use?"

"We'll see in a minute. Come on up here." And Stanley went up on the stage for a brief demonstration of the use of the enhanced visualization called Golden Images.

He was going to demonstrate for the group how the mind worked. Seated and relaxed, Stanley was asked to imagine that he was back home. He was to describe everything that came into his mind, including the clarity of the images.

"I'm in my bedroom working," Stanley began. "I've got a small office area in a corner of the room. There's a pile of papers on the desk that looks like a small mountain. It's six o'clock, Captain Kirk comes to mind, 'Star Trek' is on, now I'm watching the TV. I'm smiling."

The instructor broke into Stanley's description. "While you're in your bedroom office, try straightening out the papers and report what you're thinking about. Describe your thoughts with all the actions. Tell me if the images are clear or fuzzy, bright or dim; be as specific as you can."

Stanley was quiet for a long moment as he sat at ease with his eyes closed. Finally he said, "I'm still there. I see the pile of papers on the table. It's a mess. It's not too clear. I think the color is, well, there's no color, it's a black and white and gray scene. Bang, there's a picture of Captain Kirk, I can see the inside of the *Enterprise*. Sulu is smiling, and there's McCoy and Spock."

Again the instructor broke in, asking, "Stanley, I want you to describe the intensity of the mental image. Are the people of 'Star Trek' bright and clear?"

Stanley smiled. "Yes, they're as clear as a bell. Full color and three dimensions. I can practically touch things. And every now and then I zoom in on someone."

"What about the office images?"

He shook his head. "Oh that's nowhere, it's fuzzy, small, hazy, dim, and yukko."

"So," the instructor said, "your office image is fuzzy and small, and the 'Star Trek' image is clear and large. Now, then, I want you to put a frame around the 'Star Trek' image. Make the frame blue. And I want you to put a white frame around the office image. I'm going to count from one to three and then say 'switch,' and I want you to switch the two images. The office image will be clear and large and the 'Star Trek' image will be small and fuzzy. One, two, three, *switch.*"

The image in Stanley's mind changed. His office

was now clear and bright, three-dimensional and vivid. He was told to enhance the scene more so that the office image was not only in front of him but alongside and behind him as well. Then he was told to visualize the office neat and spotless. His office image was clear, vivid, sharp, colorful, and large. His office looked as though a tasteful decorator had just arranged everything. The "Star Trek" image in the blue frame had already disappeared.

Stanley opened his eyes and smiled. He reported that he couldn't wait for the seminar to end so that he could get to his office and sparkle it up. He fidgeted for a while in his seat thinking about his great office. He thought about it in a totally different manner. His image of the place had changed along with his viewpoint.

Then the Silva instructor looked again at him and asked, "Stanley, have you ever been on a diet?"

He nodded. "Sure, lots of times. They don't seem to work for me. I can't wait to stuff food down my throat, diet or no diet."

"Well, you're pretty good with procrastination. Why don't you use that ability to put off eating?"

Stanley once again looked confused. "What do you mean?" he asked.

"What you do when you procrastinate is to diminish the image of the activity you do not really want to do, that thing you have a small desire for, and you enhance the image of the activity that you want to do. Procrastination is always a substitution of one thing for another. The substitute is always something that you want more. You invariably will create a strong, bright image for that thing.

"Knowing that, you can use procrastination to put

off smoking, drinking, or stuffing food that you don't really need or want into your mouth.

"How about anger, resentment, jealousy, guilt? How about using this procrastination that you seem to be so good at for putting one of those things off? How about using procrastination to put all the negative things in your life aside for a while? How about putting off old age? Why not put off getting a cold, or illness in general? How about putting off things like that?

"You have a wonderful, positive resource there and you've been using it in the wrong manner. Or rather you have not been using it at all, it's been using you.

"How about putting off putting things off?"

The class laughed at that one, and Stanley smiled as the concept dawned in his mind. He was good at it. He began to understand how to use it. He really did not want to repress it. Why lose something that could be a valuable tool in your life? All he had to do was gain a better understanding of the concept of the blue-and-white-framed Golden Image, and there it was, clear as a crystal goblet.

Why not put off the bad things in your life? Procrastination—creating weak, dim images—can become a valuable resource for you. Say that something unpleasant occurred in your past that you feel bad about. The reason you feel bad about it is that you have created a strong mental image of it. You know that procrastination is creating a dim image, while the thing that you are substituting is clearer and brighter. Turn down the intensity of the unpleasant image; dim it, fuzz it, diminish it, and soon it will no longer bother you as you put off thinking about it to think instead about something brighter and clearer. That's the way the mind works. That is controlling your mind. It's a conscious effort to change the images of your mind.

Notice that when you understand the concept of Golden Images, things clarify. Isn't it the same—intensifying the mental picture of you, in the chair, feeling pain—when you are fearful of the dentist? What you do is conjure up images of pain and difficulty, thereby making the visit an unbearable experience. When that happens, you're making the wrong image golden.

Instead, put the first three fingers of either hand together (our Silva trigger device) and create an image of yourself leaving the dentist's office with your teeth repaired and a smile on your face. Make that the Golden Image while blue-framing the other one. The trick is to use the Golden Image consciously, and to know which images to diminish and which to enhance.

PART TWO

Your Mental Processes

Chapter 6

STRESS

Again and again you hear it: all of our problems are caused by stress. Books, television shows, and movies tell us the same thing: stress causes problems. Illness, indigestion, obesity, skin rashes, sleeplessness, job burnout, marital breakups, family squabbles, fights with friends, loss of employment, depression—all have been linked with stress. What's more, not only does stress cause these problems, but they in turn cause stress.

Just what is stress? It is a force of some kind, certainly—a force created by the mind that can distort, stretch, twist, compress, or deform the body in some manner. Not only are the parts of the body that we see subject to stress; so too are the unseen, the below-the-surface areas such as the organs and cells.

Stress does not affect the body alone. The mind as well is stretched, twisted, and distorted. When you are under stress, your attitudes and viewpoints are changed and things that were clear are seen as through a shimmering wave of opaque glass, clouding perceptions, diminishing self-esteem, and changing your manner of dealing with others.

When something stressful happens, the body instinctively sees it as a threat and goes into a fight-or-flight mode. In stressful situations, the mind tells the body: danger is imminent, get ready to run or to fight. Your body, unaware that there may be no real physical danger, responds to the message. Notice the changes that occur when you go through a stress-filled incident. Your shoulders come together as though to protect you, and your face muscles tighten as you shy away from the situation. You feel your chest clench, your stomach muscles harden, and the buttocks tighten. Your entire muscular system stiffens to prepare for a possible onslaught. A slight nausea sets in as the body gets ready to expel the food in the stomach so as to make it easier to run. If the threat is seen as great and immediate, the bowels may loosen. Breath comes a bit faster so as to oxygenate the blood and bring the cells to a high state of energy. Your veins and arteries dilate to allow a faster rate of blood flow to spread the oxygen more quickly.

After the initial stimulus has passed and the adrenal flow that gave a temporary surge of energy to the body to deal with the threat has dissipated, you are left in a weakened condition that further aggravates the uncomfortable feelings.

When the stress is unremitting, the cells lose their ability to reproduce. The diminishing army of cells cannot resist the onslaught of germs and viruses that cause illness and disease.

One Tuesday after a weekend seminar a woman called one of our instructors and in an agitated voice said, "I have a cold." Needless to say our instructor was a bit perplexed. Why was she calling about a cold? She was a recent Silva graduate but the instructor hardly knew her. She continued to speak saying, "I accept all the concepts; I feel so strongly about the things that you said that I just know it's impossible for me to get sick. And yet I woke up this morning and I have a cold." She paused for a moment and then asked, "Why?"

The instructor asked in turn, "Did you have an argument or a fight with your husband within the past few days?"

"Did we," she answered. "We had a lulu Thursday night. I mean it was a battle royal. As a matter of fact he left the house and didn't come back until Friday afternoon. I stewed all day Friday, but what's that got to do with . . ." She paused as what she was saying sank in. As recently as that previous Sunday she had learned that negative events do have physical consequences, especially when one gives them energy by enhancing the visual images or by constantly thinking about them. The same holds true for positive events, but that is another story.

"Of course," she said finally. "That's where it came from."

Thanking the instructor, she continued, "I just couldn't believe I attracted this thing. Isn't it funny, that disagreement was so very strong, and it just flew out of my mind this morning. I couldn't relate it to this cold. Well anyway, I'm going to get rid of it fast now that I know where it came from."

She hung up as our Silva instructor no doubt continued thinking about the seemingly mysterious consequences of even an incidental bit of stress.

As it is with the body, so it is with the mind, for stress creates not only physical problems but a Pandora's box of mental problems as well. With a weakened body and a high rate of brain-wave activity, one's relationship with all outside influences changes. This confusion leads to insecurity and a state of mind in which thoughts like "I just don't give a damn" or "Why me?" are common. A sense of victimization, self-pity, procrastination, and lassitude may set in as the person under stress finds it increasingly difficult to take a chance on what might be and procrastinates again and again. Dealing with the unknown becomes too great an ordeal, and apprehension about the future causes confusion; it seems better to leave things as they are. Thus the status quo—unsatisfactory as it may be—is reinforced, thereby setting up a state of unremitting low-grade stress.

The manifestations of this kind of stress are evident in myriad ways. If you feel exhausted for no reason, if you not only look forward eagerly to the weekend but dread Monday morning, chances are you are involved in a stressful situation at work.

If you smoke too much (a notable if questionable stress reliever) and find it impossible to stop, stress may well be the cause. If you overeat, daydream constantly, use drugs, drink too much, or shop and run up bills past your credit limit, stress could very well be at the root of your problem and you could be doing these things to relieve the stress in your life.

When you are involved with something that you do not wish to be involved with, when you have something that you do not want or want something that you cannot have, when you expect something negative to occur, then the forces of stress are ready and able to attack you.

When you do not like a thing that you are involved with and find it impossible to avoid or to change, it is likely that you are setting up a condition of unremitting stress in your life.

The feeling of simply not wanting to do anything at all is one of the most common manifestations of stress—and one that creates great havoc with relationships, in family situations, and in the workplace.

What, then, is an effective way to deal with stress? Let us propose a few ideas. First, you may prevent or lessen stress by letting go. To let go of one thought you think of something else. The best way to do this is to go to level, where you are most concentrative, and give your full attention to any thought other than the one you wish to release. When a person goes through a highly stressful period and then lets it go, he or she has a better chance of escaping from the body's manifestation of illness or disease. As with all things, however, there are different degrees of "letting go." To illustrate:

Once upon a time there were two holy men strolling down a wooded path in a forest outside Naples, Italy. Their heads were cowled and bowed, and the hoods of their robes cut much of the world off from view as they strolled along, softly mumbling their orisons. Coming to a narrow stream, they stopped. A young lady stood beside the creek. She had on a new pair of shoes and a long peasant dress and seemed reluctant to cross the stream lest she muddy the dress. Without a moment's hesitation one of the monks picked up the young woman and carried her across. He put her gently back down on the path. She smiled her thanks and he nodded in response. The two continued their walk in silence. After some time had passed, the quiet was broken by the other monk, who was obviously highly agitated. "How could you do that?" he asked, his face in a grimace of disapproval.

The first monk, deep in thought, looked at his companion in astonishment. "Do what?" he asked.

"How could you touch that woman? You picked her up and handled her, and you—you touched her." The holy man's mouth was set and compressed.

"Oh, are you still carrying that young lady?" the first monk responded, a twinkle in his eye. "I put her down an hour ago."

When something occurs that has an effect on you to the point of causing some degree of stress and you continue to think about it, to carry it around with you, you give it energy. The more you think about the incident, the greater the energization, until it does indeed cause trauma. It is vital to put the thing down.

A second and more basic way to deal with stress is to realize that the true cause of stress is not people, frustration, disappointment, fear, unfulfilled desires, or negative expectations. Purely and simply, the cause of stress is your attitude toward these things.

Once again: stress is not caused by problems. It is your attitude toward the problem that causes stress. Knowing the cause of stress makes it easier to deal with, for now the appropriate question can be asked. The question is not how can I rid myself of stress, but how can I change my attitude toward work, events, disappointments, fears, and people?

The answer is covered in Chapter 2, "Switching

Your Viewpoint to Love," which deals specifically with attitudes and how to change them, and Chapter 3, "Five Rules of Happiness."

Along with an attitude change, a change in brain-wave production will alleviate the stressful condition effectively and with immediate results. Stress causes a faster brain wave than does relaxation. When you relax, you slow your brain-wave activity. And therein lies the key.

You may face a situation so filled with stress that you do not see how you can relax, especially during the day. Or you may be under great stress without knowing its cause. Either way, the answer is the same. There is no way to get dark out of a room other than to let light in. The only way to get stress out of your being is to let in relaxation. You cannot be relaxed and stressful at the same time. When you relax for a period of time every day, you moderate stress. By moderating it you reduce its negative effect.

The form of relaxation that research, testing, and feedback from millions of people suggest is most effective is the Silva basic method of going to level. First-stage meditation, as outlined in Chapter 1, slows brain waves and alleviates stress.

To enhance the meditation still further we recommend a second stage of meditation called the Daisy Pond, developed specifically for deep, healthful relaxation. Using the Daisy Pond meditation every day not only moderates stress but also helps to change your attitude toward problems. Daily practice slows down brain waves until you can enter the ten-cycle Alpha level rapidly and easily. Eventually your state of mind changes, and the stress usually disappears altogether.

The Daisy Pond is a visualization fantasy. Read

through the description below once or twice before you practice the exercise yourself, or read through it once and then have someone else read it out loud to you as you listen with your eyes closed. Remember that you are free to use your imagination to alter any of the particular images to suit your own ideas of beauty and serenity.

Find yourself a comfortable place where you will not be disturbed. Relax, close your eyes, and count yourself to your level as described in Chapter 1. When you are totally relaxed . . .

Imagine that you are in a small hallway with a large, ornate, beautifully carved oak door at one end. Mentally walk to the door and imagine it slowly opening. On the other side of that door is the Daisy Pond.

Concentrate your full attention on the door opening. When it is fully open, you see a lovely pond. On its surface of shimmering clear blue-green water, huge lily pads float here and there. Around the perimeter of the pond is lush foliage—trees, and flowers, thousands of flowers, beyond counting, yellow and purple and green and red and violet; all the colors you love. Friendly animals are grazing, and a thirsty lion laps up a drink from the pond. He lifts his great head to look at you for a moment and then turns and strolls off into the woods surrounding the pond. To one side of the pond you sense an animal posing, watching you. It's a unicorn. Now it's your turn to stare as you focus your concentration on the stately beast. The unicorn snorts, briskly shakes its mane, and stands on its hind legs, pawing the air in your direction as if in greeting.

Taking in the entrancing scene, you become aware of a daisy in the center of the pond. It's huge—large enough for you to lie on comfortably—and so you project yourself to the center of its soft, velvet-smooth pad. Lie there for a while, your nostrils filling with the delicious aroma of the flowers perfuming the air. Imagine the clear blue of the sky above, a few white puffy clouds floating lazily by. You are still, content. Then you sit up and look around, your entire body one big smile. You see a rabbit digging a burrow, a deer approaching for her daily drink of water; she stares with soft big black eyes. A bear lumbers over and sits heavily at the edge of the pond splashing himself with the water. A few elephants playfully spray themselves while a baby elephant trots around them, trunk held high in the air, squealing with delight. After a while you slide over to one of the petals and ease yourself into the water. The temperature is just right, and you float on the buoyant surface and then swim for a while.

This is the true fountain of youth and health. Drink deeply of the water, and you begin to feel better and better—aglow with health, strong. Then dive below the surface of the pond and swim underwater. There are many beautiful fish there, all friendly. Play with some of them. A dolphin appears, greets you like an old friend, and swims alongside playfully. The water of the Daisy Pond is like air—you can breathe it. Feel the water go through your circulatory system, cleansing and purifying your blood. The stem of the daisy looks different from an underwater perspective, almost like a grand redwood. Swim around it, the dolphin accompanying you.

After exploring the underwater world in complete comfort, swim to the surface and project yourself back to the center of the daisy. In the distance you can see three mountain peaks, one of them covered with pure white snow. Here in the land of the Daisy Pond the mind can do wonderful things and so you find yourself levitating up, up, up, like Peter Pan. You hover over the pond, flying around its perimeter and smiling at all the animals as they drink, eat, or just play with one another. The flora look different from this perspective, as do the pond and the daisy. Now you head toward the mountain peaks, glimpsing the plains below as you fly. A great herd of buffalo appears, and then an eagle comes close and flies alongside you for a few moments.

When you reach the snow-covered peak, you land feetfirst in the snow and play there for a while, drinking in the crisp, clear air. You slide down a hill, and when you reach the bottom, you soar up in flight once more to circle the peak. Then you fly back to the daisy and sit in its center, soaking up the languid warmth of the air. You are tranquil.

Now project yourself back into the hallway. Imagine the great door closing, and count yourself out of level.

We have found this exercise to be one of the most effective ever developed for overcoming the negative effects of stress. We recommend making any changes you like so long as the basic premise is there, that of concentrating your attention on a controlled, stress-free, relaxed fantasy of your own making.

But this is only imagination, some might say. True, but consider that fear is imaginary, resentment is imaginary, stress is imaginary; all the emotions, both positive and negative, are imaginary. They are created by the image-making faculty in your mind. You might say that your reality, your world, is imaginary, for your reality is the product of your attitudes, your viewpoints. What we are doing with the Daisy Pond exercise is getting your imagination to work with you instead of against you. After all, you and your mind are on the same team. It is necessary for you to work together.

Chapter 7

To understand courage it is necessary to comprehend the emotion called fear. Basically there are two types of fear. The first is genuine fear, fear felt because of some genuine threat. Fear is a necessary tool for survival in all animals. It responds to danger by giving the individual a chemical smack of adrenaline to jolt the body into instant action. When you pass a dark alley late at night, the fear you feel that someone might jump out at you helps make you faster, more focused, and stronger. The fear helps you to get away from danger immediately.

However, fear that was designed long ago to prepare a person for a physical act in the forest is not necessarily appropriate in the workplace. An executive, say, learns in a meeting that he or she may soon be fired. The thought of losing a job would create fear in most of us. But what kind of physical act or reaction is proper in this situation? What should be done in response to a nagging worry that could last for weeks before it is resolved?

Obviously, there is nothing on the physical level that can appropriately be done. Yet the physical component of fear, a residue of our prehistoric past, still persists: adrenaline flows, circulation is redirected within the body, and so on. Prolonged fear (often known as unremitting stress) can actually damage the body.

Although the fear itself may be valid, the instinctive response it elicits is often out of proportion to the threat. It is impossible to program out that response, since it is one of our strongest instincts. So we can only deal on a practical level with its longer-term effects.

Before we get into that, however, let's take a look at the second category: illusory fears.

Illusory fears, though just as genuinely felt, are based upon misperceptions, on false commands emanating from a person's inner tapes.

Many people spend their lives in a constant state of anxiety and have no idea where it originates from. Others suffer from phobias—greatly exaggerated, distorted responses to something perceived as a hazard. Illusory fears are the bane of their existence.

Illusory fears often stem directly (and occasionally indirectly) from an inadequate self-image. The ego, or sense of self-esteem, may not be up to coping with the complex problems of modern living, and the natural reaction to this is stress caused by anxiety. If the self perceives itself as inadequate to cope, anxiety, always waiting in the wings, is all too ready to pounce and take over. An inadequate sense of self generally, if not always, stems from childhood programming by an authority figure.

Illusory fears are often based on misperceptions. Say you open your door one day to find a snarling dog ready to leap and bite. You back up so quickly that you trip over your own feet and fall down. But the dog doesn't jump. You take a second look and discover that the dog is a mop you had left on your front porch the night before. Because it was not what you expected to see (the usually clear porch), your mind did not recognize the mop but startled you into a self-protective mode just in case there was danger. There's no danger, of course, from a bit of dark wet cotton, but a dog, yes; let's see a dog just in case we need protection. And when you see the dog instead of a mop, all the defensive reactions of the body spring into place and back you go.

The misperception was quickly cleared up. That was easy. Many misperceptions, however, are buried deep in the subconscious, and in most cases they've been programmed by well-meaning parents or other authority figures. Beliefs, attitudes, and the ways we see things are our perceptive resources, some of which work to our advantage and some of which do not. What we as individuals accept as truth, our perception of things, belongs to our overall belief system. Some of these belief systems can be quite resistant to recall. No one ever remembers something that happened in its actuality, but only what happened as perceived by that individual. That perception is affected by mood, emotion, age, company, environment, and even the weather. The same experience that two people may undergo will later affect each in a totally different manner.

Reprogramming illusory fears to convert them to positive expectations enhances one's awareness and self-esteem. As the self-esteem improves, one in turn becomes less and less prone to react to illusory fears.

Aside from improving self-esteem, how can you handle illusory fear? First, let's try to gain greater awareness by defining the word, using the principle of polarity. When you examine the opposite meaning of a word, the concept that you are attempting to understand is unlocked, leading to more awareness. To define the word *fear,* we go to our polarity gauge and lay it out with a negative pole on the left end and a positive pole on the right. We would call fear a negative, and under the word *negative* put *expectation.* On the right end of the polarization gauge would be the words *positive expectation.* It might also be termed *faith.* Fear and faith, then, are the same, differing only by degree.

Fear is a negative expectation. When you are fearful, you are expecting something bad to happen. Once you are aware of this, it becomes easier to deal with the fear. You simply change the negative expectation to a positive expectation. It is not difficult to do this; it requires but a bit of practice.

To eliminate a fear, polarize it: switch to a positive result of the thing you fear. Take, for instance, our example of the executive who is about to be fired. The first reaction might be to visualize the difficulties of a reduced income and the lessened prestige that would likely accompany the dismissal. But what are the positive aspects of losing the job? Our executive might think of a period beyond the immediate difficulties and start to see this as an opportunity to do what he or she really wants to do—perhaps to move to another area, switch fields, or explore any number of attractive possibilities not previously available.

Another benefit of changing your viewpoint is that it helps you identify and develop your desires. When you hold a positive desire, the result is usually a positive expectation. And, as we've just seen, a positive expectation—faith—serves to diminish a fear.

You might initially think courage, not faith, is the opposite of fear. But consider that courage exists only where there is fear to be overcome. Without fear there can be no courage; you would just act. To ask yourself why you are fearful leads nowhere because fear is an abstraction. Better to ask yourself what you expect of a negative nature to happen; then you begin to close in on a useful answer.

Perhaps an even more fruitful question to ask would be this: what would you be doing if you did not expect this negative thing to happen? Suddenly all kinds of positive answers come into view. Fear is imaginary just as faith is imaginary—and both being imaginary, they are subject to your mental control. You can control fear by changing it to faith. And this is the technique that we use for eliminating fear—to transmute, or change, the fear.

In considering your debilitating fears, ask yourself the question, "What would I be doing, and what would my life be like if I did not expect this bad thing to happen?" Now you are transmuting, for your imagination brings into play all of the positive possibilities, and at last you have a weapon to fight the fear.

Fear is a necessary part of the systems nature has installed in us. If we were to wipe out fear from a person's environment, we would be doing an injustice, for the trigger of fear is often necessary to remove you from harm's way, should danger arise. However, illusory fear, illogical fear, fear in which the fight-or-flight response is not required can only hamper one's growth. So identify your fear. Is it necessary? Is fighting indicated? Is running involved? If not, in all probability it's a fear that you do not need.

To deal with it, go to your meditative level. Polarize the fear; visualize the positive expectations. What would you be doing if you did not have the fear? Go over this again and again. Use the Golden Images techniques introduced in Chapter 5 to enhance the positive image and weaken the negative. Symbolically smash or erase the negative image and do not concern yourself with it again. Whenever you consider the thing, visualize only the positive, beneficial results.

If flying is your fear, visualize the positive aspects of the trip you're taking. Visualize yourself sitting comfortably on the plane. Picture a safe, smooth landing and the successful outcome of the trip. Imagine the things that you would be doing happily if you did not have this fear.

To dominate your fear, you change the negative expectation to a positive expectation. You do this with your viewpoint, at Alpha, through meditation. You do this with that part of your own mind that rules the world, your imagination.

Fear is imaginary, courage is imaginary. The source of courage is in the imagination—your image-making creative ability. Herein lies the ultimate wellspring and true source of courage.

Chapter 8

GUILT AND SELF-FORGIVENESS

In Chapter 3, "Five Rules of Happiness," you learned that the first rule of happiness is "If you like a thing, enjoy it," and that there are only two reasons not to enjoy something you like: fear and guilt. Having dealt with fear in the last chapter, let's examine guilt.

More than any other emotion, guilt puts a heavy burden upon us both spiritually and mentally. Guilt has been laid upon our shoulders by many authority figures—by parents, teachers, and friends; by the media; by our government and our educational and religious institutions. This burden of guilt is placed on us for two reasons: to control and to punish.

To understand guilt better we must first be aware of what precedes and what comes after guilt. For guilt is part of a threesome, accompanied by two fellow travelers, sin and punishment. Let's define all three words.

Sin is a missing of the mark. Guilt is a compulsion

to repeat an act correctly. Punishment is a reminder that comes along when the act is not repeated correctly.

A brief story illustrates how this trio works together. Helen M. had been brought up to believe that kissing a boy the first time she went out with him was wrong. Helen is now twenty-two years old and has forgotten that the original programming of this belief came from her mother when she went to a friend's birthday party at age eleven. On every date she is very careful to keep to her "principles," and does not allow even the most innocent of kisses.

If she were to remember the incident of the birthday party, she would recall that although excited, she was apprehensive as well. Her mother was to drop her off at her girlfriend Arlene's house and leave her there. There were to be a lot of strange boys attending, and this was the first time she had ever attended a mixed party. As her mother laid down the rules to protect her little girl, Helen felt a mild confusion about the entire event. (Apprehension and confusion provide a perfect breeding ground for programming.)

"Now Helen, darling," her mother began, "I want you to remember that you are a pretty little girl and some of the boys are going to want to kiss you."

Helen's eyes opened wide as her mother spoke. She drank in the words from this great authority figure, the source of all the good things in her life. Every word was accepted as gospel as Helen concentrated, staring into her mother's eyes.

"If any boy tries to kiss you, you are to walk away from him. Do you understand that?"

Helen nodded solemnly as her mother continued,

"What are you going to do if a boy tries to kiss you, darling?"

"I'm going to walk away from him," Helen responded, emphasizing each word with a nod of her head.

Her mother smiled and patted her little girl. "That's right, dear, walk away. Remember this always, Helen. Never, ever, allow a boy to kiss you the first time you meet him or on the first date. Remember that and you will always be all right."

And so the line was drawn, the mark set. It was sinful to be kissed on the first date.

One day, many years later, Helen meets her dream man and out the window fly her principles. They not only kiss but go in for some heavy petting as well. She has missed the mark that had been set. She has shattered the commandment set by the great authority figure in her life, her mother.

There's the sin (so far as Helen is concerned), but where is the guilt?

The next day Helen wakes up with a smile on her face. But then there is a nagging feeling of having done something wrong. She feels uneasy and her mind is split. On the one hand she feels wonderful, on the other terrible. She starts thinking things like "Loss of respect," and "How could I allow that?" She tosses and turns in her bed as she analyzes the previous evening.

Time passes and the fellow doesn't call back. Helen was all right, but he has many other women friends and she was just an incident in his life, already forgotten.

But Helen doesn't forget. She is now convinced that

82

he did not call again because of the terrible sin she had committed in allowing him to kiss her on the first date. (That's her programming, remember.) And now guilt enters the scene. "Why did I do that?" she thinks. "If only I could undo it." But how? The more she thinks about the incident, the more energy she gives it to strengthen the guilt.

There are many different methods that Helen can use to punish herself for being a bad girl. She chooses food. (Note: All the avenues one chooses to punish oneself are below the level of consciousness.) Subconsciously she decides to fatten herself up to make herself unappealing to men so it will not be necessary for her to tell them she will not kiss them good night. If she makes herself unappealing enough, there will not be many dates with good-looking men and it will be easier for her. She begins a regimen of eating high-calorie foods and puts on more and more weight. In the meantime, on the conscious level she is thinking, "I must go on a diet, I look horrible."

She goes on a dozen diets but nothing seems to work. Finally she rationalizes her new look by thinking something like, "Well, some people were just born to be overweight." She doesn't realize that she is caught up in the progression from sin, to guilt, to punishment.

This story is, of course, an oversimplification meant to serve as an example. We must remember that our present society seems to admire the emaciated look seen on so many fashion magazine covers. Other countries and other times have considered a bit more meat on the bones to be more desirable (look at a picture of the queen of the 1890s, Lillian Russell) and healthier. We picked weight as an example only because so many people are weight conscious. Beauty is in the eye of the beholder, after all.

This example can be seen as symbolic of many other guilt-producing situations. What would the kiss represent in your life? And what would be your equivalent of overeating?

Now let us examine the trio from a different angle, one component at a time. First there is the sin.

An outside agency, such as a parent, an institution, a peer, the government, or the media, sets a mark for you, telling you that this is the way it must be. If you do not follow the rules that are being laid out for you, it is implied, then you are doing something wrong and you will be punished for it. Generally these rules are set before a young and growing mind, the type of mind that is most receptive to information. Upon hearing these rules from the great authority figure, an impressionable child accepts them as valid information, and so all the "thou shalts" and "thou shalt nots" take root. And when the young person does something that violates a rule, it feels as though he or she has done something wrong—has, in fact, sinned.

And then there is guilt. Nature has installed within the human framework a great many fail-safe systems, such as intelligence, self-awareness, and guilt. When we feel that we have missed the mark, that we have done something wrong (sinned), then we experience what has been placed there by nature, a compulsion to repeat the act, but this time correctly.

It is not possible, however, to repeat most sinful acts, from the simple sins of eating something that you were not supposed to eat or failing to be nice to your mother's brother when you don't particularly care for him, to a host of complicated "shalts" and "shalt nots" that have been set by outer agencies. These guilts or compulsions to repeat begin to build and are ultimately released in a punishing action. Unfortunately, the punishment does not necessarily fit the "crime," nor does it absolve the individual.

Punishment is simply nature's little reminder, her way of saying, "Say, you didn't do that correctly." How strong is the punishment? That depends on the margin by which the individual feels he or she has missed the mark; it is totally relative to the individual. On the physical plane (and we're not relating this now to spiritual sin and guilt), a person killing a butterfly may feel more remorseful and carry a heavier burden of guilt than the same person would killing a human being. For that individual the killing of the butterfly is the greater sin, if he or she believes it to be a greater sin. For most of us, the reverse would be true, but in any event the degree of punishment sought is relative to an individual's guilt.

Just as surely as night follows day, guilt follows sin and punishment follows guilt. When the guilt has not been released, then the reminder, punishment, enters the scene, usually in the form of limitations. Individuals with guilt piled upon burdensome guilt tend to limit themselves in life, feeling "I only deserve X . . . ." I only deserve so much money. I only deserve so much good health. I only deserve so much in the way of a home, of a spouse, of friends, of clothing, and so on. These are self-imposed limitations that the individual is scarcely aware of, all stemming from unresolved problems in one's life.

Sin and guilt are imaginary in that they stem from the imagination. They're mental. Punishment is mental as well, the difficulty being that it manifests on the physical plane, thereby causing many problems.

How can you neutralize guilt? To neutralize guilt, you polarize it and switch your viewpoint. In this case we're neutralizing the negative effects of guilt. The negative effect of guilt is a condemnation of one's self. The opposite of self-condemnation would be self-forgiveness. Therein lies the key to overcoming guilt.

How easy.

How difficult.

It's easy to say Forgive yourself. But before forgiveness must come understanding. Know that whenever you do something, whatever it is, you are doing your best *at that time.* We always do our best. At no time do you ever go out and say I'm going to do the worst I can. Even when you want to do something badly, you still do your best to do it badly.

Say that somebody you respect asks you to do something, you agree to but don't, and then you feel guilty about it later. At the time you didn't do it there were reasons you didn't. They may have been subconscious, or they may have been conscious, but whatever they were you can bet that reasons did exist. Given the same emotional state, given the same circumstances, the same mood, the same you, given the same opportunity, you would have done (or not done) exactly what you did (or did not do) the first time around.

The very fact that in the present you might feel you had done something wrong in the past is a measure of your maturity. You have grown, you have evolved, you are more aware, you are more mature. Of course, the new, mature you looking back at some past error, some past missing of the mark, can say, "That was dumb, why did I do that? I wouldn't do that today."

Of course you wouldn't do it today. You're not the same person you were then. With your greater awareness and maturity as resources, you recognize the thing now as an error you will not commit again.

Know this: whatever you do, you do your best. Whatever you did in the past, given your resources of that time, could have been done in no other way. There's nothing to feel remorseful about. There's nothing to feel guilty about. The fact that you do feel guilt is an indication that you have grown to the individual you are now. You may forgive yourself for all of your past "errors," for you are a different person today.

Forgive yourself, for you could have done it in no other way. Forgive yourself, for you will not do that again; you are more mature.

If twenty thousand angels with twenty thousand Bibles in their hands were to attest to the new you and forgive you for all your past misdeeds, yet you remained unforgiving of yourself, then you would not feel forgiven. On the other hand, should the whole world condemn you and you forgive yourself, then you would feel forgiven. The key lies within your own imagination, for this is where guilt, sin, and punishment reside, in that image-making capacity of your mind. Imagine that you have forgiven yourself and you will be forgiven.

Michael G. was a successful building contractor until the roof fell in on him one day and he had to declare bankruptcy. Many problems were created by this failing, but as it turned out the one that affected him the most was guilt. He felt enormously guilty that his wife and three children would not have the things he had promised them, and was wretched because their lives had changed so much. He went into a state of depression so deep that at one point he felt that his family would be better off without him and seriously considered suicide.

How does this example fit our definitions? Michael had set his own goals in this case, but his will to succeed had been established while he was still a child. His parents had programmed him in grade school that the most important thing in life was good grades and that he must get A's if he was to have their approval and entire love. Michael was a good student and soon developed a strong need to succeed.

When the bankruptcy occurred, he had indeed "missed the mark" that had been set ostensibly by himself, but actually by his parents many years before.

Because of his family's change in life-style, he felt a great need to repeat the episode again, this time correctly so that he would not go into bankruptcy. The need to repeat the act correctly is, of course, guilt. But alas, he could not. The business was gone. And because he could not repeat the act correctly, the last member of the formidable trio came marching onto the scene. Punishment reminded Michael that he had not corrected his action. Michael felt helpless and out of control. Feeling that he could not do a thing about the situation, he contemplated the ultimate punishment, the taking of his own life.

On top of all this, stress came into Michael's life and he felt listless and drained. He put things off and became a real burden to his family. He became argumentative and morose, keeping more and more to himself, withdrawing by degree into a shell of help-lessness.

This describes Michael the day before his wife,

Marcia, dragged him into one of our Silva Mental Dynamics seminars. Marcia related the story three months later. Michael took to the meditative part of the course immediately and began going to level three times a day. He analyzed his problem and realized that he had set impossible marks for himself, coming to the conclusion that he was competing with his parents' conception of success, not his. He was competing with the wrong person. Because his mother and father had made him fiercely competitive, he always looked to his peers to see how well they were doing; if any of his fellow contractors was doing better, he was dissatisfied with his own efforts and so was never really content, always wanting more. He wanted to be the biggest and most successful contractor in the world.

Suddenly he realized he had set the wrong goal. He should have been competitive with the only person it makes sense to compete with, himself. Now he set out to be the best Michael G. that he could, and that he could still do. It didn't really matter whether he was a big and successful contractor; if he was, that would be all right, but if he was not, why that was all right as well. "As a matter of fact," he said later, "I thought, why should I be a contractor at all? I never really enjoyed it."

He went to level to examine all aspects of his life. He asked himself what he enjoyed. It seemed that the only enjoyment in his life was golf. He loved golf but seldom got a chance to play. How wonderful it would be if he could pursue some occupation that involved golf. But best of all, he realized that he did not want to go through it all again, he did not care to "repeat the act." And he could forgive himself, for he realized that he had done the best he could with the tools he had at the time. Finally he put his burden down. He let it go.

"It's really strange," he reflected recently. "There I was without a cent. No prospects, no money, no house, no car, forty-four years old, and happier than I'd been for as long as I could remember. I had made up my mind, I was going to get a job at either a golf shop or a golf course, and it didn't matter what kind of job it was, I didn't care so long as it was golf.

"My friends must have thought I was nuts, but I didn't care. I was lucky, though; Marcia went along with everything. I went to work for a country club in Los Angeles. It was a menial job but I went into it with my eyes open, determined to do the best job I could. I was going to be the best me I could be, and I was. I've been working there three months now and I must say that they've been the happiest three months of my life. I'm not making that much money and Marcia went to work, but she picked a job she enjoys as well and we're closer now than we've ever been. I go to level three times a day and I'm happy. No man can say more."

It warmed us to hear Michael's story. He is now setting his own goals and he will be the better for it; but most important, he has forgiven himself for all his past "misdeeds."

The way to neutralize guilt is through self-forgiveness. To forgive yourself you must understand that the you of today would not act in the same way as did that past you. If a particular incident is hampering your growth, go to level and review the event. Go over it thoroughly just as you remember it happening. Put a blue frame around it and compress the frame until the scene is diminished. When the frame compresses to the size of a bean, imagine it disappearing in a *poof!*

Bring the event to mind once again. This time imagine how you would act with your present resources. Picture the incident with the actions of a new, more mature you. White-frame the scene and focus on it. You can forgive yourself because you have grown to a new awareness (proof of that is the guilt you felt about the incident in the first place), and with awareness comes the realization that you wouldn't handle the event in the same way again.

You are your actions. You now have new actions and are a new you. While at level, put the first three fingers of either hand together and say, "I forgive myself for all my past actions. From this moment forward, I will be the best me that I know how to be." When you come out of level, live your life the best way you know how. Be the best you that you can be.

Chapter 9

ANGER

All things have their opposites. Many are obvious: day as opposed to night, hot as opposed to cold, tall versus short, freedom versus slavery, love versus hate, and so on. To understand the nature of the one, it is always helpful to examine the character of the other. Could there be a better way to understand freedom, for instance, than to have been enslaved? A tall man does not really understand tall nearly as much as a short man does, and vice versa. Who appreciates warmth so much as those who have been chilled? Water to the thirsty is far different from what it is to the drenched. The natural and the unnatural, fear and faith—these and virtually all other things are opposites, differing only by degree, and by reflection and consideration we can identify their polarities and shed light on their natures.

What would be the opposite of anger?

We know that anger is a negative reaction, as well as

a feeling of great displeasure. So the opposite would be a positive reaction and a feeling of great pleasure. The opposite of anger is pleasure. If we were to imagine a gauge with anger on the extreme negative end and pleasure on the extreme positive end, we would find that at the halfway point is a neutral zone that is neither pleasure nor anger, but simply total noninvolvement, an area of neither negative reaction nor positive reaction, but of no reaction at all.

As you move by degrees from the extreme negative end toward the center of the gauge, there is less and less anger; once passing the center neutral zone and moving into the positive section, there is more and more pleasure.

What is it that gives you pleasure? What is it that angers you? In both instances you will find that they are reactions to some stimulus outside of yourself. Re-action. Because anger is a reaction, you are the one responsible for it, for you are the action and the reaction. You are your actions. To change yourself, change your action. Once you understand this, change—even from displeasure to pleasure—becomes possible.

Let's look at the anatomy of anger through the eyes of Bunny and Bully. Bunny has a weak sense of self-esteem. His poor opinion of himself has created a weak ego. Bunny's poor sense of self makes him feel that everyone is on the attack. (If he thinks so little of himself, how can anyone else think much of him?) And so he angers easily. Everything that anyone does or says is sifted through this belief of being unworthy. Even something as inconsequential as "Hey Bunny, I see you bought a new coat" could infuriate him. He feels that the coat hangs poorly, it's cheap, the color's wrong, the salesman talked him into it; all stemming from the negative opinion of himself that carries over to much of what he says and does. His reaction to the simple remark is to become angry. "What's it to you?" Or, "You don't like my coat? Go take a flying leap at a rolling doughnut." And the friend who innocently commented on Bunny's new jacket walks away dumbfounded.

People with low self-esteem anger easily, because their reactions are generally of a negative nature.

And then there is Bully, the typical aggressor who walks around with a chip on his shoulder daring people to knock it off, praying for reactions to his constant aggressive attitude. He fears that he is less than others, that other people are better than he. Wanting to feel as worthy as anyone else, he belittles other people, imagining that if they are smaller, he must be bigger. And the smaller and weaker he sees others, the larger and stronger he feels.

Bully seeks out Bunny and calls him a name that indicates that his mother slept in a kennel and his father was worse. Bunny seethes with anger. His reaction to Bully's words are out of proportion to the words, which have no real meaning or significance. Bully does not even know Bunny's mother and Bunny knows this but his sense of self is being attacked and he feels as though he must react, if nothing else to show his manliness. If he really felt like a man, with the knowledge that he was equal to every other man, if he had a good opinion of himself, he would not have to show his manliness. He would *know* that he was a man. When you know something, you do not have to prove it to anyone, least of all to yourself.

But in this case Bully is much larger than Bunny, more confident of his fighting abilities, stronger and better equipped for physical action. Bunny is cowed. He doesn't dare fight back, much as he would like to, and so the anger turns inward. He hates himself for not responding the way he would like to. He sees himself as cowardly, as inadequate to handle the situation, and his opinion of himself goes down another notch.

What would Jack Armstrong—secure, confident, typical high-ego individual—do in a case like that? Would he react by getting angry? No. Would he fear being called a coward? Why should he? He knows that he is not. In all probability he would treat the incident as if a strange dog were barking at him. Why should he react to a stranger telling him something that he knows is untrue?

Take another instance that goes beyond mere talk. Jack Armstrong is backing his car into a spot and accidentally bumps against Bully's fender. Bully's reaction is immediate and violent. He yells, "You stupid ass, look what you've done to my car!"

Actually nothing has been done to Bully's car, but it seems to him a perfect time to bolster his flagging self-image once again. One more opportunity to make someone small in his eyes.

Jack instantly realizes the type he is dealing with. Just as he would attempt to go around a barking dog, he goes around the aggressor. He says, "Say, I'm really sorry, it was an accident."

But Bully will have none of it. He complains about his bumper and the idiotic way that Jack drives and possibly even throws in a few views as to his parentage.

"How can we settle this?" Jack insists. He just wants to soothe the barking dog. After the realization that he is not going to cower, Bully gets into his car and drives off. The last thing in the world that he wants is for the person in front of him to show more strength than himself. That would lower his self-esteem even more, making him more of a bully than ever.

Jack has been, on our imaginary gauge, right on the neutral zone, reacting neither in a negative manner nor in a positive manner. Jack did not react at all. Indeed he took an action—the action of getting out of the predicament as peaceably as possible. But this was an action, one that he was in control of, rather than a re-action, an action that he was not in control of.

Think back to any time when you were angry and you will find that you reacted to some stimulus outside of yourself. Know this for a fact. You do not have to react to anything unless you want to react to it. For the most part we are programmed to react, we are hypnotized into thinking that a response in kind is called for or we are not mature adults. Actually the mature adult is the one who thinks before reacting to anything.

Let's take another case, one involving not physical confrontation but anger at an inanimate object. Bunny goes out to his car after shopping and finds that someone has dented his fender. He searches for a note or some indication of who has done this dastardly offense but finds nothing. He throws his bag of groceries down on the ground and curses a blue streak for five minutes. He bangs his fist on the fender and looks around the parking lot, boiling with frustration and anger. His stomach churning, he finally gets into his car and roars out of the lot. On the way home he yells at everyone and blows his horn to get people out of his way or to hurry them up. Needless to say his dinner that evening has been ruined, his family suffers, and he tosses and turns all that sleepless night as he envisions the person who dented his fender undergoing all kinds of torture. A negative reaction to the sight of the dented fender.

But, you may think, the sight of a dent in a fender would cause a negative reaction in anyone.

Not so. The totally confident and mature person, with high self-esteem and a healthy ego, would immediately see the situation for what it was. First of all, the dented fender was not an attack on the self, it was an accident. After looking around for a note and finding none, the mature person would shrug it off and think about other things, not reacting to the fender dent and therefore not making it a problem.

Then there are those who not only are mature but can use the Silva Mental Dynamics method to turn the situation into a positive one. Those who react, but in a positive manner. The positive reaction is one of pleasure. How, you may well ask, can any sane person react with pleasure to the sight of a dented fender?

Recall the story of George S. and his dented fender, recounted in Chapter 3, "Five Rules of Happiness." George had turned a dent into an advantage. Seeing the crimped fender, he thought, "I wonder what it will cost to fix that dent? Whatever the cost is, I will set a goal to make three times that amount in the next few months." When the body and fender shop gave an estimate of $250, George set out to make $750 over and above his normal income. Instead of focusing on the no-good lowlife so-and-so who caused the dent, our Silva person is thinking only about how to make $750. Every time our Silva person sees the dent he thinks, "Five hundred dollars extra in my pocket," and smiles. A positive reaction.

And so we've seen three responses to the same situation. Bunny's negative reaction, Jack Armstrong's neutral action, and a Silva graduate's positive reaction. Can you imagine how each of these three people goes through life? Can you imagine how each of them feels about himself and about other people, other things, experiences, and life in general?

You might ask at this point how you can change your anger and frustration, if not to a positive response, at least to a neutral one. Let us offer you a few simple Silva techniques for ridding yourself of anger, or at least cutting it off before the reaction begins. The first is the three-finger technique introduced in Chapter 1. Simply by placing the first three fingers of either hand together and saying "calm" or "forgive" during an episode in which you would normally react negatively, you will find yourself remaining calm and collected so that you can deal with the problem in a mature manner.

One other technique for stemming anger before it begins is called the feeling-good switch. If you place the tip of your tongue at the center of the inside of your top front teeth and slide it up until you reach the gum line, you will find a point where the gum dips down just a bit. That is the feeling-good switch. Whenever you are in a situation in which someone's anger is about to cause you to react in a negative manner, just touch the feeling-good spot with the tip of your tongue and think the word *calm,* and you will switch yourself to calm, or remain calm and in control of yourself.

All emotions are imaginary in that they are of a mental nature. Anger, like all emotions, creates a visual image that stimulates the reaction. The techniques outlined in this chapter as well as in Chapter 5, "Golden Images," will give you the imaginative wherewithal to quell the imps of frustration, displeasure, and resentment—and, of course, the negative reaction of anger.

Chapter 10

SELF-ESTEEM

What is self-esteem? It is a confident feeling you have about yourself. You might say that self-esteem is ego, that part of you that assesses who you are.

What do you think of yourself? Do you have a high opinion of yourself, a good regard for you? Then you have a good, strong ego. If you have a poor opinion of yourself, and little regard for you, then you have a weak ego.

It is possible, of course, to have different opinions of yourself in different areas of your life. You may have a good, strong opinion of yourself in one area, and think rather poorly about yourself in another. Unfortunately, the poor opinion is generally the one that is focused on—the old homily of the squeaking wheel getting the grease. So what do we do to overcome this?

The first step is to understand that *self-esteem is your opinion of yourself.* Once you appreciate this, you are well on the road to strengthening that self-esteem.

Next, ask yourself why would you have a poor opinion of yourself in any area of your life? One reason might be that you have compared yourself with other people. If you come up short in that comparison, your opinion of yourself is diminished and problems arise.

What you must do is to enhance your opinion of yourself. But how? When you compare yourself with another person—whether that person is an artist, attorney, plumber, secretary, senator, nuclear physicist, musician, sportsman, or whatever—if you feel that he or she is better than you in any particular area, your general opinion of yourself will be diminished. The only faithful way in which to look at other people so that you have an accurate feeling about yourself is to see those people in the most general way, in a way that puts everyone on equal footing.

Consider that everyone has different resources. Not everyone is a man, not everyone a woman. Everyone is not tall or short. Everyone is not overweight or underweight or normal. But everyone *is* a human being, and in that regard you are equal to every other human being. You are not equal to a horse. A horse is much stronger than you. But you do not feel diminished when you acknowledge a horse's superior strength. A dog is faster than you, but you do not feel diminished because the animal can outrun you. An elephant is larger than you but you do not feel diminished by that. The horse, the dog, and the elephant are outside the realm of the generalization of what you are, a human being.

Some people see other human beings as having attributes they lack and feel shortchanged. This feeling of deficiency, even in but one area, shows up in your overall ego, in your general opinion of yourself. When everyone is seen as a human being, then everyone becomes equal. Tall, short, rich, poor, knowledgeable, ignorant, overweight, underweight, or average—these characteristics are irrelevant. We are all human beings, and seen in that light there is no competition. For there can be no competition. You cannot enhance your position as a human being, nor can you diminish your position as a human being. You are, have been, and always will be a human being, and you know that for a fact.

When you see other people as human beings, you begin to realize that every human being on earth can do things that you cannot. You can do things that no other human being on earth can do. That does not make other people greater than or lesser than you. It simply makes them different in particular aspects of their lives. Are they better for it? Perhaps from their point of view they are. From your point of view they are no better, they are simply different.

Take a look at two trees. Say that one is a thousand-year-old redwood, a great stately tree. You look at it and then look at a small, stunted pine tree trying to grow through a crevice in a mountain rock. Do you see the redwood tree as better than the pine tree? Of course not. All you see are two trees, and that's all you should see because that's all they are. One is larger, the other smaller, but better doesn't enter into it in the slightest. When you see two people, whether one has an outstanding talent or not, what you're looking at and what you should be seeing are simply two people. When you are indeed able to see two people, and there is no competitive urge to be better than either one, then you have reached a high level of self-esteem and can see yourself for what you are in fact—a human being, equal to all.

Everyone has something. What do you have that no one else has? Think about that. There is something you can do that no one you know can do. Does that make you better, or does it simply mean that you can do something better than anyone else?

Is there anyone in your life you look up to, anyone you feel is better than you? Then you should work on enhancing your self-esteem. Is there anyone in your life you look down upon, anyone you believe is less than you? Then again, your self-esteem needs work. When you see everyone, from those you formerly looked at as the lowest of the low to those you viewed as the highest of the high, as equal to you—doing things differently perhaps, but all equal as human beings—then your level of self-esteem is healthy.

When you have high self-esteem, you are in constant competition with the only person it makes sense to compete with—yourself. Life then becomes a game, and all the things in life that were bothersome become challenges and part of the game.

The story of Charlie B. serves as a good example of the benefits of competing with oneself. Charlie, a carpet installer who attended a Silva Mental Dynamics class, was constantly trying to do better and be faster at his job than anyone else, without success. After the SMD seminar he decided to compete with himself. His job at the time was laying carpet in a new development of tract houses. For the first time in his life he brought a stopwatch with him. He timed the installation of carpet in every room. The bedroom took him one hour, the hallway two hours, the living room an hour and ten minutes, the stairway two hours and thirty minutes. He finished the job, noted all the times, and carefully placed his notebook in a pocket.

The next day he felt more enthusiasm for his work than he had in some time. He pulled out his notebook and stopwatch and began, his goal now different from what it was before. Now his goal was to install the bedroom in less than one hour, to install the hallway in less than two hours, to install the living room in less than an hour and ten minutes, and to install the stairway in less than two hours and thirty minutes. Before he knew it, the day was over and he had cut thirty minutes off his previous time. He fairly bristled with anticipation of the next day.

It wasn't long before Charlie was the fastest carpet layer in his shop. And then he decided to go for the perfect job. He would attempt to make seams invisible and perimeters perfect. After he achieved his new goal he sought out the more difficult jobs. After Charlie became the top mechanic in the shop, he decided he would open his own shop. He started a modest establishment and solicited a few accounts. He decided to continue with the game of competing with himself. When he got an account, he determined to get a better one the next week, and a bigger one the week after. Within two years Charlie had the largest carpet installation shop in the country. Needless to say his self-esteem grew along with his business— mainly because Charlie decided to compete with himself.

Whenever you set a goal and accomplish that goal, your opinion of yourself is enhanced. This is true whether it is a long-range goal, an intermediate goal, or a daily goal. Goals that are self-competitive are easily attained, since all you are striving for is to do something a bit better or faster than you did the last time. The accomplishment brings about a satisfying feeling and an immediate ego enhancement. You can accomplish many tasks working with a stopwatch to compete with time and yourself. Other tasks would call for a different measure of competition, challenging you to improve your level of relaxation, or the number of charitable acts you do each week, or your compliance with goals you've set, and so on.

You're okay just the way you are. Understand that all you have to be is the best you that you know how to be. Do your best at all times, even though there will be times when your best is a one and other times when your best is a ten. That's what being human is: being affected by the swinging pendulum of rhythm. There is nothing to feel guilty about when you can't quite put forth your best possible effort; the best at that time is good enough. Realize that you are always being affected by forces beyond your control, from past experiences to the weather. What you can control are things like your attitude, viewpoint, and emotions. The Silva Mental Dynamics material will help you to control these mental forces.

Nothing on earth strengthens self-esteem more than winning. Winners invariably have a strong sense of self-esteem. This ego strength varies in different aspects of your life. You may have a strong ego in one area, like business, and a poor opinion of yourself in another, like public speaking. Hence it is misleading to conclude that a person's self-esteem reflects an overall picture. In what aspects of your life do you feel you have the strongest self-esteem? What can you do better than almost anyone else? What is it in your life that you feel you can be most successful at? If you were to become even better at something you already do well, you'd find yourself feeling like a winner, your self-esteem improved enough in that realm to strengthen your ego in all realms.

The first step in our technique for improving self-esteem, then, is to pick something in your life that you are good at and want to improve. It could be cooking an omelet, playing the stock market, running a business, throwing a football, or choosing the right clothes for yourself; there is something that you excel at. Once you have decided what that is, go to your meditative Alpha level and examine it in all its aspects. Create a visualization, an image of yourself doing this activity, and then enhance the mental picture. Make the image brighter; make it larger and more colorful. Give it depth, three-dimensionality. Bring in other senses. After examining your talent thoroughly, come out of level and consider how you can compete with yourself so that you will be even better at it. It is helpful if you have chosen something that you can improve either by quality, quantity, or time.

Now to compete with yourself to improve your talent, start by setting the improvement as a goal. First, set a base line: determine how you do it at present. Then determine in what way you wish to do it better—to do it more or less, faster or slower, larger or smaller, whatever applies. Now go to your level and see yourself doing this activity better. Go through the same enhancement you used when you examined the talent before, but see yourself doing it better. Finally, set your goal to actually do it that way. When you come to an outer conscious level, hold on to that image, work toward that goal, and keep at it until you are successful. You will compete with yourself and you will be successful. Soon you will develop the habit of success, of winning, and your self-esteem will grow.

Frances G. always felt like a loser. She didn't like her features or her job, and she couldn't seem to attract the right kind of man. She came to the seminar primarily because she heard that it might help her get out of the rut that she was in. Frances had a rotten opinion of herself and listened eagerly to the seminar presentation on self-esteem and ego.

Frances chose photography as the thing that she felt she could do better than anyone she knew. None of her friends or acquaintances seemed to have the knack, and so she decided to do that better. At the time of the seminar she was pretty good, she said. But she was determined to be better.

When Frances reported back some time later, she was hardly recognizable. Her clothes, her makeup, her hair, the way she carried herself—everything was different. She seemed totally in charge. When she spoke, she came across like a leader. We asked her what had happened. She smiled and said that she had developed an idea that had come to her at level. She'd worked on it, getting better all the time, until she not only had excelled at her hobby, but had gone into business successfully for herself.

She said that at level she saw a photograph she'd taken of a mountain, except that it was different somehow. When she came out of level, she found the picture and glued it onto a heavy piece of cardboard. She then cut the mountain portion out, put a cross brace on the back of it so that it would stand by itself, and stood it on a shelf. She now had a small sculpture of a mountain. After a few days the entire shelf was filled with a range of these photo mountains. She was simply enhancing her hobby until a friend came over to visit one day, saw the unusual photo mountain sculptures and asked if Frances would do the same for her except with cactus. She would pay Frances for her time. Frances made the cactus photo sculpture and the friend sent another friend until Frances, who was now spending all her spare time with the new development in her life, tripled her prices to keep business away. Her business increased. She tripled the price again, but still she had more work than she could handle.

When we last heard from her she had quit her regular job, hired three people to help her, and started making more money in a month than she had previously made in half a year. Her self-esteem had soared. Frances showed up at a recent seminar to tell her story and say that everyone has something he or she can do better. And so can you.

What is your hobby? How can you enhance it? What do you enjoy most? How could you turn it into a business? Go to level, enhance your images, and imagine that you have developed a new use for the things that you do best. You may come up with the next hula hoop, pet rock, or Apple computer. But even if you do not, the knowledge that you can will help to enhance your self-esteem.

PART THREE

Programming:
Past, Present, Future

Chapter 11

PAST PROGRAMMING AND REPROGRAMMING

What is your purpose in life?

What do you hope to achieve with your life?

What do you see as the end result of your life?

Now consider your goals and hopes. Are they your own, or are they the result of other people's expectations? If they are not your own, could it be the result of programming by outside agencies, such as parents, religious and educational institutions, friends, teachers, governments, or the media? Has their programming set you on a different path from the one you desire to be on?

Measure what you do and what happens to you because of your present actions. Assess these events: do they further or hinder your life's goals?

You have been blessed with the gift of free will; intruding on that free will, however, are the overlays, the patterns that have been set by other people. Past programming influences your belief systems—what you are, who you are. Beliefs—the frames of reference by which you live—come from authority figures and are based on trust for those figures, who are generally your parents. Since a belief allows you to accept only information that supports that belief and causes you to reject information that contradicts it, maintaining beliefs programmed by others is giving up your free will. For if you can only accept information that supports your belief and if that belief was formed by another individual, then it is not you creating your reality but in fact that person who installed the belief in you.

If your life and your life-style are the way you wish them to be, then the past programming has been good for you and you would not wish to change it. Consider this. Are you satisfied with where you are in life at the present time? Consider your positives, the good things in your life. Consider the negatives, the bad things in your life. (Actually things just are; there really are no bad or good things, there are just things. They become good or bad as they relate to you. It is your perspective, your attitude, your viewpoint that makes them good or bad. Fire is good when it cooks your food, terrible when it's burning down your house. Rain is wonderful for the farmer who needs irrigation and terrible for the poor guy drowning in the swollen river nearby.) But what of your own positives and negatives? Do the good things outweigh the bad? Consider your present life as objectively as you can. What is your opinion of your life as it is at present? You might say what we're looking for here is a life ego as opposed to an individual ego. Your individual ego is your opinion of yourself; your life ego would be your opinion of your life as it is up to the present time.

If you're not satisfied with your life, if your opinion of it is negative, then it is possible that past programming is one of the reasons. Let's see if we can break the barriers that keep you where you are. Let's discover whether or not you can become more aware of the person that you can be, the person that you'd like to be. The first step is to rid yourself of past programming instilled by others. The second step is to reprogram yourself according to your own goals.

Past programming is a dam holding back the natural free flow of your life stream. Just as a river is programmed (controlled) by means of a dam—built by agencies to direct the energies of the river to their advantage—so too do outside agencies direct and control you through programming.

To rid yourself of unwanted past programming, sit in a comfortable place, go to level, and visualize the dam as your own programming blocked, going no place. Imagine the dam as representing all those beliefs that are preventing you from achieving what you want. Release this body of water by visualizing the dam breaking up and the waters of the lake being released to flow once again as a river. The free-flowing water represents your *own* thoughts, your *own* mind. Your thoughts, free to flow as you direct them, suddenly allow you to be in control. You may not be able to control your beliefs if you imagine them as absolute but you can control beliefs when you realize that you have the ability to do so simply by directing them. Your mind will be under your control. Outside agencies will make suggestions but it is up to you to accept or reject any future programming.

After the visualization, consider making a change in your life. First, make a pact with yourself regarding any future attempts by outside agencies to program you. Close your eyes for a moment right now and repeat these words: "I will only react to constructive suggestions." As you repeat the words, concentrate on them. Hear your voice speak each word.

Next, prepare to determine your own programming. Consider what it is that you'd like to change in your life. Programming sets energies to work for you (your own programming, that is); it sends messages of energy out into the universe. Visualization strengthens that energy and lends wings to it. What is it that you're not satisfied with? Where would you like to be? You're the controller now and now is as good a time as any to reprogram your life. What kind of life-style would you enjoy having? Visualize yourself with this life-style. Visualize yourself enjoying this life-style.

Reprogramming is simply setting yourself down on another road so as to travel in a different direction. If you're not satisfied with your present life, it is possible that you are on the wrong path. Imagine that you're standing at a crossroads, where different roads in front of you lead to different places. Visualize the different place each path leads to. Visualize the end result of the path you're currently on. Picture which road leads to the place that you wish to be.

How do you get on the right road? You make a change of some sort. It may be a major change such as moving, or not moving; buying, or selling; changing jobs, or staying put. Or it may be seemingly minor, such as changing your eating habits, or cleaning up your home or office. But whatever the change is, you make it and life gets a little easier. If life does indeed become more satisfying, then obviously you are doing something right. This is a message that says, "You're getting the idea, keep doing what you're doing." If you do it again to enhance the change and life gets better still, that too is a communication to you—a message that you're doing things right and should continue what you are doing.

Chapter 12

PROGRAMMING YOUR GOALS

Most programming techniques described here work in a similar way: you visualize what you do not want and erase it, and then you visualize what you do want, imagining the result after it happens.

When programming for some goal that you wish to attain, you are sending out a message to the universe that you either want something you do not have or wish to rid yourself of something that you do have. This message travels in much the same way as a television or radio program is transmitted. The station sends out waves of energy. The wave of energy travels in all directions until it reaches a receptive device of some sort, a radio or television set. Providing the frequency or amplitude of the waves and receptor match, there is a fitting, and the program manifests.

So it is with your own programming. When you program using the various techniques of the Silva

Method, you must be in the outgoing mode (as described in Chapter 24, "Communication"). When you receive, you must be in the receptive, incoming mode. Constant programming will keep you in the outgoing mode. As long as you are transmitting, you cannot receive. You must place yourself in the receptive mode at some time to receive the result you are programming for. Expect it to happen and it is more likely that it will happen. As with so many facets of life, the injunction "Ask, and ye shall receive" is much more effective when carried out at the ten-cycle Alpha level of mind.

One of the most versatile and effective programming techniques in the Silva repertoire is called Center Stage. You may use Center Stage to gain something that you want, or to rid yourself of something that you do not want. Consider for a moment what it is that you want. Think about the end result only. Do not contemplate how to go about getting to the end result; imagine only having achieved it. If there is something standing in the way of that achievement, think about that as well. When you visualize yourself with the positive outcome of your programming, visualize the date you wish the action to take place by.

Here is how the three-act Center Stage technique works.

Go to level as described in Chapter 1. Then visualize yourself outside a theater. Walk into the theater and take a seat in the third row center.

Act I. Imagine that the curtain is closed and you are sitting comfortably. When that picture is set in your mind, visualize the curtain opening and then project yourself onto the stage. Bring people who are involved in the problem onstage as players in the drama. Imagine the scenery, the setting; bring in appropriate props. Now act out your problem. After going through the scene, project yourself back to your seat and visualize the curtain closing. When the curtain is closed, mentally write a big red NO on the curtain and mentally say, "Any past feelings that hold me to that scene, I now release." Sense those feelings departing from you, and note how you feel when rid of them.

During the second act you are going to set the pattern to make the way easier for yourself. Most successes are preset patterns. The more you do something, the easier it becomes. Your goal in the second act is to remove all limitations from you so that you can go beyond your normal abilities, and most of all to set the pattern for success. During the second act of Center Stage you will use an alter ego to smooth the path for you.

Think for a moment: if you could choose any personality, living or not, real or fictional, to represent you in a play about your life, whom would you choose? This player will be your alter ego and will act out the solution to your problem during Act II of Center Stage. You have already determined the positive end result of your program; during Act II you will remain in third row center while your alter ego acts out the scene. You are the director as well as the author, and you may mentally change the action at any time.

Act II. The curtain opens. Your alter ego is playing your role. You begin the action. Visualize your alter ego being successful at whatever you are programming

118

for. See the action. If you're programming for a new job, for example, see your alter ego in the new job, sitting at your desk or performing your duties on a stage set to represent your desired work environment. Have the players act out all of the activities of your goal accomplished. Now bring in a target date: hear a voice saying, "This will happen by [target date]." After setting the date, close the curtain. Mentally write on the curtain the word BETTER, and mentally state, "This is the way I want it to be."

Now that the pattern has been set, the only thing remaining is to do it yourself, and that is when Center Stage Act III comes in. During Act III you will play out the scene in exactly the same way as your alter ego did. The pattern has been set. You bring in the same date. This time, however, you will project yourself into the scene and you will act out the positive end result of your program accomplished.

Act III. The curtain opens. You project yourself onto the stage and act out the solution to your problem in the same manner as did your alter ego in Act II. Bring in the same target date. After acting out the positive end result with yourself playing the starring role, project yourself back to your seat in third row center. The curtain closes, and you mentally write on the curtain, *better and better,* and you mentally state, "This is the way it will be." That is the Center Stage technique.

We recommend doing Center Stage three times for each one of your goals. Run through Center Stage once each day for three consecutive days. On the first day perform Acts I, II, and III; on the second day, do only Acts II and III; and on the third day, perform only Act III. Act I is visualized only once for each problem. You want to concentrate on the solution.

Attending one Silva class was Barton E., a gentleman who had recently gone through a bankruptcy and for a year had languished at home feeling sorry for himself. A friend brought him to the Mental Dynamics seminar, and he showed some interest in a few of our ideas. But the Center Stage programming exercise was, he said, "a bit too far out to accept."

That was fine with us, since many of our instructors had been skeptical themselves when first hearing of such techniques. We do welcome skeptics as long as they have an open mind and will take a wait-and-see attitude. Barton was skeptical, but he participated in the Center Stage exercise, programming as his end result a thriving business and a new car (specifically, a gold Cadillac Eldorado).

He wasn't sure what business he wanted to be in so long as it was not his old one, and so for his end result he visualized himself sitting in a plush office and speaking on the telephone, his feet up on the desk (only the boss puts his feet on the desk with impunity). He also saw himself signing checks, going to the bank, and taking delivery of his brand-new gold Cadillac Eldorado. He visualized himself being admired in his new car and mentally saw all the positive actions of a successful businessman.

He did feel a bit foolish doing the exercise, he said later, but he considered the fact that millions of people all around the globe have been using the Silva Method for problem solving and programming for more than twenty years, and he decided to take a wait-and-see attitude.

He called us some four months later to report with excitement, "It all happened. Everything! I can't figure it out. It doesn't make sense to me, but here I am in my plush office, head of a successful business— and oh yes, I have a gold Cadillac Eldorado in a parking spot with my name on it in the lot."

Barton E. brought more than forty of his friends to the class after that, and his success story was repeated by many of them. Programming works. Try Center Stage for one of your goals.

Chapter 13

PAST SELF, FUTURE SELF

People often think about some past event and say with chagrin (or worse, guilt), "Now, why did I do that? That was stupid." And with head shaking and face drawn in a frown, they spend long minutes, hours, and sometimes days and weeks in mental self-flagellation. If the guilty thought gnaws deeply enough, they may spend months or years in consternation and regret. When looked back on as stupid, past things that were once done or not done, said or not said, accomplished or not, started or never begun, wind up with a lifetime of punishing limitations.

Logically they should not. Why should a past event have the energy to wound a present you? Why should a past event have the energy to weaken or sicken you? Why should a past event have the energy to destroy families, relationships, business ventures, occupations, professions, and people themselves? What gives a past event this great power to control the destiny and thoughts of an individual? For past events do have this power. Past events can create havoc not only with a person's mind, but with the physical body as well.

You have power to change your attitude toward a past event here and now. Yet in actuality there is no now, only a continual flow from past to future, for "now" is already in the past. What we know of as now is the past of the future and the future of the past. Because there is no now, we can work wonders when we seek to change the future by looking to the past.

Thought knows of no time, no space. You can think yourself on the dark side of the moon in an instant. You can go back to a past event, whether hours or centuries past, in the blink of an eye. Thought is limitless, with the exception of those thoughts that are limited by one's self. Through the use of directed, dynamic thought, the past can be changed by modifying your conception of the past.

All problems created in the present were born in the past. These problems obtain their power from your image-making faculties known as imagination. Your directed imagination can reverse many negative situations in your life when understood and properly used.

If you feel that you've done something stupid in the past, you are probably familiar with the wish, "If only I could go back to that incident, I would certainly do it differently."

No you wouldn't. Consider this: you always do the best you can. Given the same you, the same emotions of that time, the same situation, and all your resources of that time—your knowledge, the state of your health, your mental state, energy level, and so on— and the ability to travel back, you would do it exactly the same way again. If you feel at present that you did something stupidly in the past, and if you regret having done it, that is a measure of your maturity. If you had not grown, you would feel the same way that you did in the first instance. The present you has different resources from those the past you had. These resources include your expanding awareness, your greater intelligence, more knowledge, and certainly not the least, the fact that you are looking back in retrospect and already know the result of the action. Taking those resources back to the past incident would create a different you, a better you.

You are the result of all the past events of your life. However, it is not the events that have constructed the present you, but rather your attitude toward those events.

Let's take an example of two people and see first, what made them the way they are, and second, if they can change the way they are should either of them desire to make a change. We will consider a confrontational, hostile personality, and a congenial, friendly one. Let's name the confrontational person "Hostile" and the congenial personality "Friend."

In the case of Hostile and Friend, a crossroads had developed in early childhood, a place where two separate futures could evolve, depending on the action of the moment. When they were twelve years of age, there was a confrontation between Hostile and Friend, and this was the incident that set up their egos toward the particular aspect of their lives that are in question. (Ego, you will recall, is one's opinion of oneself.)

Something was said by one or the other, and Hostile

challenged Friend to fight. Friend refused and Hostile got angry, called Friend a coward, and yelled, "Go home to Mama!" Friend shrugged and walked away, confused and depressed.

A simple incident. Let's look at the mental imagery of Hostile and Friend at the moment in question.

Whether consciously or subconsciously, before you take any action, an image is created in the mind. If you reach for a glass of water, you have reached for it first in your mind. Sometimes only an instant separates the image from the action, and sometimes longer periods of time, but a visualization always precedes an action.

During the time of confrontation both Friend and Hostile had visualizations. Friend's mental image was that of defeat. Hostile yelled "Let's fight," and Friend's mental picture showed Friend lying in pain on the ground, in the dust, with nose bleeding, and then running home and crying. The mental image was that of classmates laughing, pointing fingers, and walking away. With such images, of course Friend did not want a confrontation with Hostile. Mentally, Friend was already defeated; the way for those images not to manifest was to refuse to fight, and so Friend turned and walked away.

Hostile's images, however, were quite different. Friend was lying on the ground with Hostile standing over a beaten opponent. Hostile visualized the whole school looking with awe on the great Hostile's fighting ability and bravery. Hostile visualized walking proud, shoulders back, head up and smiling, the hero of the school. No wonder Hostile became aggressive. Hostile wanted those images to manifest into reality.

As they grew and matured, much changed. Friend was not really cowardly as an adult, but whenever there was a confrontation, Friend tended to back away from it as the images (images, incidentally, that Friend was unaware of) tended to the negative, defeatist side. The reverse was true for Hostile, who had a tendency to jump in with both feet and take charge of every situation. Friend tended to take everything apart, studying and turning things over mentally for weeks before making any decisions at all, whereas Hostile just did it.

There is no judgment here as to which one was better off as an adult, since there is something to be said for each type of personality. What we are getting at is that neither of them has any knowledge at all as to the workings of the mind and both of them are somewhat out of control.

When you understand the mechanism of the mind, you can control your life better. Sometimes you want a touch of the negative so as to avoid disappointment, or to view the situation from a different perspective, to take it apart and see all its facets. At other times you want to jump right in, and that takes a positive attitude. When you are aware, you are in control. And that is the key, control.

Neither Friend nor Hostile turned cowardly or heroic during that particular incident at age twelve. Much preceded it, but the incident was a key factor. It was a crossroads in both their lives, and both of them recall the incident with ease. Hostile, when thinking about it, gets warm inside and laughs; Friend gets a chill, shrugs, and feels a mite uncomfortable even as an adult. Both recognize the incident but attach no importance to it.

When Friend thinks about the incident as an adult, the memory plays tricks and Friend doesn't quite remember exactly what happened. Was there a bloody nose, a crying youngster? Or wasn't there? The intervening years have changed Friend's memory of the incident to a large degree, as have the years changed Hostile's recollection.

Because the incident did not actually happen the way Friend thinks it happened, Friend can, with a simple Silva Mental Dynamics technique, switch viewpoints toward the incident. Of course when the incident is changed mentally—via the switched viewpoint—the chain of events that has instilled a defeatist attitude in Friend is also changed. For to change the incident that made Friend into a person Friend considers overly timid and self-effacing is to change the attitudes that stem from the incident as well.

But you might well say, you can't change something that already happened. Yes you can. Because nothing ever happened the way you think it happened. It is not possible to have an accurate, objective memory; your past programming and beliefs always color the reality.

Every experience you have is filtered through your resources at that time and seen through the lens of your attitude. If your memory involves a person, it is not actually the person you see but only a projection of the person, a projection that person is putting out. It is as though you were looking at a shadow thrown on a wall by the person and, thinking the shadow image is the individual, directing all your attention to the shadow. All people project this shadow image— many, even to themselves. True feelings are always hidden below the level of consciousness. Hidden because most of us are fearful of bringing them out into the open, even to ourselves, much less to others.

The way that Friend thinks about the incident is actually false. It did not happen that way at all. What Friend has done is to create a memory of an event that Friend believes affected all subsequent attitudes toward men, women, business, and life in general. New confrontational incidents trigger Friend's recall of the childhood confrontation with Hostile and stimulate the attitude and actions of the original episode.

And so, to change a past event, you simply change the memory of the event. You do this by changing your attitude toward the event, going back in time to redirect your past frame of mind.

This is how it works.

Say that Friend was in a Silva Mental Dynamics class. Friend would be instructed to go to level, or meditate, using the three-to-one technique as outlined in Chapter 1. Once at the Alpha level Friend would go back in time to that crossroads and instruct the past self in the proper use of the mind. Present Friend's resources are vast as compared to the resources of the twelve-year-old self, and present Friend can lend those of a future self to the past self.

Friend visualizes the past event using the Golden Image technique to enhance the picture. The scene is brightened and made more colorful. Friend now makes it three-dimensional and senses the depth of the scene. Friend gets an idea of the odor of the past scene, the sound of it, and the feel of it. The action is stopped.

Still at level, Friend mentally strolls over to the past

self and opens a line of communication by introducing the present self. Friend tells past self that it is present self from a future time and that future Friend is going to help past Friend by lending past Friend some of future Friend's resources. The resource that future self is going to give to past self is that of mental imagery. Past self is going to change the mental image of the impending conflict.

Now confrontation is about to take place. Hostile has just yelled at Friend, "Let's fight." The action is frozen, like a still picture, but Friend's past self has mobility. Friend's present self is sitting comfortably at level and with great imagination is creating the scene. Operating as a future self, Friend now imagines standing in front of the past self. Friend tells the past self what has happened, explaining that the fear stems from the mental pictures that past self has been creating. But now, because future self is lending past self the resource of knowledge about how the mind works, the past Friend can handle the confrontation.

Past Friend is told by present Friend to change the images, to picture past self laughing at the idea of fighting and to realize that the only result of a fight is that Friend or Hostile or both will be hurt. Past Friend is told to visualize a scene in which Hostile is chagrined by Friend's refusal to react to taunting and slinks away. Past Friend is given an entirely new set of mental images. Now friends and classmates are offering their congratulations on the manner in which the confrontation was handled. Friend visualizes boys and girls thinking how courageous and wonderful Friend is, standing straight and tall. Friend changes and sees past self as a popular and respected student in the school. Present Friend—still at level—makes the scene brighter, larger, and more colorful. Finally Friend puts a white frame around the entire scene, and it becomes Friend's new memory of the incident.

If the old scene of past Friend running away ever intrudes on present Friend's memory, a blue frame is immediately clapped around it, and Friend reverses what was done with the white frame. Friend takes the color out of the scene, makes it flat and one-dimensional, makes it smaller and smaller again until the scene is as small as a bean, and then sees it disappear. Friend then brings up the white-framed scene and enlarges it, making it three-dimensional, bringing in sound, odor, touch, taste, and other things to enhance the reality of the scene.

Now whenever the incident comes to mind, Friend's thoughts are about the newer incident involving the wise and mature past self. And after viewing the event a number of times, Friend develops a new memory and attitude, letting go of an entire string of events once seen as negative. A newly dynamic and confident Friend is born.

If you have a problem with any aspect of your life that you feel was instigated by some past event, you too can go back to that event and change your attitude toward it by going to level and willing yourself back to that time. Speak to your past self and explain who you are; explain that you are wiser, have more resources, and intend to help set your past self on the right path by showing that past self how to use the mind to be rid of all negative forces. Explain to your past self how the mental images create fear, anxiety, and stress. Explain how to change the mental images to control the situation. And then have past self—under the guidance of your present self—make the necessary changes.

PART FOUR

Empowerment

Chapter 14

DESIRE, BELIEF, AND EXPECTATION

How can you influence events so that they go your way? How can you solve problems you face? How can you change the things about yourself you're not satisfied with? While there's no disputing the fact that you can't always get what you want, it's also true that you *can* exercise enormous influence over the events of your life and make things go your way much more frequently. To do so, you must understand and use the three mighty forces of desire, belief, and expectation.

Before anything you want to happen can occur, you must *desire* that it happen. You must *believe* that it can happen. And you must *expect* it to happen.

Let's look at each of these three forces and then see how you can put them to work for you.

Every manifestation of will is preceded by the desire to act. You must desire something before will can take action. In order to desire something, you must believe that you will gain a measure of satisfaction from it.

Anything you do, from the moment you wake up in the morning until the time you close your eyes to sleep in the evening, is precipitated by desire. Nothing is done that does not have a degree or more of desire behind it.

The satisfaction you feel you'll gain from any action can be either the direct satisfaction of pleasure or the indirect satisfaction of the avoidance of pain. When you have several competing desires, the most likely choice will be the one that gives the greater measure of satisfaction. Sometimes it appears that a choice may offer the lesser amount of satisfaction; if that is the case, then look for a secondary gain.

Visiting the dentist for a root canal, for instance, hardly appears to offer great satisfaction. The secondary gain in this case is the elimination of the pain in the tooth. Elimination or avoidance of pain is often a secondary gain. Another secondary gain might be the attention of others due to an episode of discomfort, in which case the attention would more than compensate for the discomfort.

Avoidance of pain keeps a good many people stuck in a particular position in life simply because they feel that making a change would cause some measure of discomfort. To avoid the discomfort they linger in the existing state of affairs even though that causes discomfort as well. The sayings "Better the devil I know than the devil I don't" and "Don't jump from the frying pan into the fire" express this sentiment. Note the system of expectation at work here. When discomfort or pain is expected, the force works to keep you from making any change, even when the pain is imagined and may never take place.

Like all things, desire has degrees of strength. Consider the story of the disciple who went to his guru one day and asked, "Master, how do I achieve enlightenment?" The wise old guru directed the disciple to the bank of the Ganges River and had him kneel with his head over the water. Then the guru put his hand on the young man's neck and pushed his head below the surface of the water. After a minute and a half the young disciple was frantic. He pulled and heaved and flailed his arms, but the grip was like iron. He could not get his head back out of the water. After two minutes, when it seemed as though his lungs would burst, the grip was released. The young man's head jerked out of the water and he took great gulps of air into his tortured lungs.

The guru smiled. "Tell me," he gently asked, "what was your greatest desire just then?"

"To breathe," the young disciple stated emphatically.

"Ah," the guru said. "When you desire enlightenment to that degree, it shall be yours."

To have a better understanding of desire, see it on an ascending scale, like a giant thermometer. At the bottom of the scale is zero, and at the top, one hundred. When your desire is weak, near the bottom of the scale, it is unlikely that anything will motivate you to activate your will and accomplish the object of that desire. When your desire is near the top of the scale, there's almost nothing that can keep you from success in attaining that desire.

How to enhance desire is discussed in Chapter 18,

"Motivation and Procrastination." For present purposes, let us propose three rules.

Rule #1: To enhance desire, go to level and visualize the positive end result of what you desire to happen. Bring in Golden Images; make the scene brighter, larger, more colorful, and three-dimensional. Bring in as many senses as you can. You will find your desire for the event growing stronger with each visualization.

Now to the second force, belief. Belief is mental acceptance of some idea as being true. You accept ideas from others because they are authority figures, and you are used to their ideas.

This setting of a belief in your mind (usually at a young and trusting age) comes about because you have absolute trust in the authority (generally the parent, sometimes the religious or educational institution, sometimes another trusted outside agency such as a relative, peer, or the media). This acceptance can come about even when there are facts that contradict it.

Reinforcement of beliefs strengthens them until, faulty or true, they become a fundamental part of your thought processes. To entrench matters more, new beliefs are tested through the structure of the faulty belief, thereby compounding the problem. What this means is that you only accept information that reinforces the belief. Information that contradicts the belief is rejected.

And here lies one of the major problems of mankind.

All bigotry, racism, egoism, and just about every other prejudice you can think of stems from ideas that have been introduced by an outside agency and accepted by the individual. Of course there are also group beliefs, some valid and some faulty.

The power of beliefs to shape one's behavior and judgment is shown in the following story. One of our Silva instructors, Marsha C., was presenting the Silva Basic Lecture Series Children's class to a group of Los Angeles youngsters ranging in age from seven to eleven years. The main thrust of the seminar is to instill in all the children a sense of their own worth, to teach them that they can do or be anything they have a desire to be, to enhance their self-esteem, and to turn them into good students by showing them there is no such thing as a stupid child, only ones who believe they are. We have found that a good student can learn more from a bad teacher than a poor student can from a skilled teacher.

This particular class had twenty children attending, one of whom, eight-year-old Jane B., believed that she was stupid. Her mother thought she was stupid, as did many of her friends. Her mother told Marsha she'd be very grateful if anything could be done for the child, although she didn't really believe it was possible in only three days.

During the class Marsha tore off a piece from a sheet of paper and told the class that it was a receptor, for it was going to receive something. She then took a penny from her pocket and placed it on the paper, putting the paper with the penny on it next to a vase on her desk. The class resumed. The next morning she asked, "Where did I put the penny?" No one remembered; too much had happened since.

Marsha pointed to the penny, still on its piece of paper next to the vase. She then tore two sheets of paper into a hundred pieces, took two rolls of pennies

139

from her purse, and proceeded to put a penny on each piece of paper and place it somewhere in the room. She told the class to note that each penny was being placed on a receptor. Soon the room was packed with pennies resting on small pieces of paper. Later on that day she asked, "Where did I put the penny?"

Everyone looked at her quizzically. No one was quite sure what she meant, since wherever they looked was a penny sitting on a small piece of paper. They were on the floor, the desk, chairs, the windowsill, in front of the door, on each table—everywhere. Finally she said, "Come on, let's all find a penny. Gather them up."

Soon every child had four, five, or six pennies. Marsha asked, "How come you all found pennies this time and you didn't find the one I put by the vase yesterday?"

"Because there were lots of them today" was the response.

Marsha nodded, "Yes, because there were lots of pennies on lots of receptors.

"Information you put into your mind is very much like the pennies," Marsha continued. "Information is stored on receptors in your brain called neurons. Each neuron holds a bit of information; that is what makes it a receptor. When you put the information on one receptor, it's hard to find it and you think that you have a bad memory, just like trying to remember where the single penny was. But when you put the information on a lot of receptors, it's easy to find."

The children didn't quite understand, and so Marsha said that she would demonstrate. She distributed a sheet of paper to each child in the room. On the paper was the story of the Battle of Trenton. Its gist was this: On a snowy Christmas day in the year 1776, General George Washington, along with twenty-two hundred troops, crossed the Delaware River, attacked an army of hired mercenaries, the Hessians, and won a crucial battle of the Revolutionary War.

Marsha called eight-year-old Jane B. aside and said, "Come with me, Jane, I'm going to help you."

Jane was insulted. "I know how to read."

Marsha smiled. "I know that, but I'm going to help you to put the information in the story on more receptors. I'm going to show you a new Silva way to read."

In Marsha's office she had Jane close her eyes and visualize the story. Jane saw a picture of Washington in her mind's eye. She felt the snow coming down. Marsha told Jane there were twenty-two hundred men in the army that day and had Jane visualize an owl, "because it's got two big round eyes like two zeros," with a twenty-two on top of its head. When it came to the Hessians, Marsha hissed because they were the enemy, and turned the hiss into the word *Hessian*. Marsha had Jane enhance the visual images: the snow was made whiter and colder; the owl was heard to hoot and was made three-dimensional; the twenty-two on top of the owl's head grew until it filled the scene; the Delaware was seen to be wearing ice. Marsha helped Jane to produce Golden Images.

They went back to the room and Marsha retrieved the story from each child. Later that day she asked, "What year was the battle fought?" Many knew the answer and raised their hands high. "What was the name of the general?" All of the hands went up. "What day was it?" Most knew that it was Christmas day. "How many men were in George Washington's army?"

Only one hand was raised. Jane B. looked around, saw that hers was the only hand in the air, and immediately pulled it back down.

Let's stop here for a moment and get back to that business of belief and the fact that you only accept information that reinforces your belief. Jane believed that she was stupid. Her mother believed it and her schoolteacher believed it. Most of the people who came in contact with Jane believed she was stupid and expected her to react in a stupid manner, as she herself did.

But did her being the only child out of twenty students who knew the answer reinforce her stupidity? It did not; it contradicted it. And so she rejected the information and down came the hand. She could not believe that she was the only one with the right answer. Marsha, of course, knew that Jane had the answer because the owl with the twenty-two on its head was a strong visual image. After a bit of persuasion Marsha finally got Jane to say, "Twenty-two hundred?"

Marsha nodded and told Jane that she was very good to have the answer. Jane now wondered why no one else in the room did, since the image of the twenty-two was so strong. Maybe everyone else was a bit stupid. A few more questions came and many in the class knew the answers, as did Jane. Then Marsha asked, "What was the name of the enemy army?"

Again only one hand went up. The answer was clear in Jane's mind. "Hessians," she stated clearly. Jane's belief began to change. It had to. To retain the old belief that she was stupid would have been to reject obvious information. Marsha saw to it that new information got through so that Jane either had to reject the information, which she had a tendency to do but which Marsha would not allow to happen, or she had to break down the old and install a new belief. The new belief was that she, Jane B., was not stupid; she was in fact highly intelligent but had been putting information in her brain the wrong way, not using enough receptors.

Her mother was told of the incident and immediately changed her belief about her child's intelligence. (When she believed Jane was stupid, she occasionally imagined her daughter as a frumpy adult, washing dishes at a filthy sink with a bedraggled child hanging on to her apron string. With the new belief in Jane as intelligent and alert, her mother's mental images changed. She now saw Jane as a college student, as a professional woman, as the mother of sharp-witted, intelligent children.)

This story took place nine years ago. Jane's mother calls us occasionally to inform us of her daughter's progress. It does not surprise us to learn that Jane has been a straight-A student for so long that she no longer relates to the incident that caused it.

Let us now propose Rule #2: To enhance or to change belief, recognize that belief is mental acceptance of some idea as being true, and that such mental images can be changed.

You can reject a belief that is causing you harm, creating problems, or limiting you in some manner. Once you have recognized your faulty belief, think about its opposite. You may not be overweight because you overeat; you might just overeat because you believe that you are overweight. Visualize the opposite. See yourself at the weight you desire yourself to be, and believe that you can attain that weight. You do this by going to level and seeing yourself active, vigorous, and at the weight you wish to be. The same process can be used to reject any harmful belief.

And now to the third force, expectation.

Expectation is a mighty force indeed—so much so that a doctor can take an inert pill and tell a patient that it is a powerful drug, and the patient will react as though the actual drug had been taken. This well-documented phenomenon is called the placebo effect. It might also be called the "expectation effect."

Of course, the placebo effect does not work all of the time. If it did, no one would bother with drugs at all. They would simply use placebos. It does, however, work with a significant and measurable percentage of success.

Expectation, a powerful force in one's life. How can you use expectation as a force in your life? Can you simply expect good things to happen, and they will happen?

When you are told something by an authority figure you respect—say, a doctor, a teacher, a parent, or your boss—those words have an effect on all three levels, the physical, the mental, and the spiritual. When you believe this authority figure without hesitation or reservation, then that person's expectation of you is more likely to come to be. With respect to your own expectation of yourself, however, you might well tell yourself, "I'm going to expect this to happen" only to hear a small voice inside respond, "Who are you kidding?" The trick is to make yourself your own respected authority figure.

Expectation is enhanced with Silva Mental Dynamics techniques that entail going to one's Alpha level and creating the visual imagery of the desired event already having taken place. This technique has a dual effect: it puts you in the position of acting as your own authority figure, and it reinforces your experience of yourself that way. The more successful you become using the Silva Method, the more you believe in yourself and the better you become at triggering the anticipated positive result of whatever event you are trying to bring about.

And so Rule #3 is this: To build expectation, go to level and visualize the event as already having happened. Use the technique of the Golden Image to enlarge the image of the event; brighten it, make it three-dimensional, zoom in on different areas of the incident as you wish it to be, make it more colorful, and bring in other senses such as hearing and feeling as well. When you come out of level, think about the event as coming about by a predetermined date. You will find more and more expected events coming to pass.

To help you change your expectation, recall the principle of correspondence—as above, so below; as below, so above. As it is with the seed, so it is with the tree. Start with the small if you want to affect the large. If you wish to bring about a change in a friend, in a parent, child, or spouse, change your own expectation. Begin to expect that which you desire to happen and you will notice changes occur.

Expect things on a smaller scale at first, and as the smaller things come into being, almost like magic, you can make the major things occur. Expectation is one of those things that can and should be discussed with the other party. Expectation works with all people, and on all levels—on the family level, on the town, city, and country level, on the national, international, and universal level. The law is the law; what works with the small works with the mighty. What works with the molecule works with the universe. Change your expectation and see your reality, your world, change to the degree that you wish it to change. And eventually you will arrive at the place you wish to be.

Chapter 15

POWER WORDS

A few decades ago, there lived a Russian psychic whose reputation for accomplishing strange and mysterious feats rivaled that of our greatest magicians. It was said that while magicians used tricks to accomplish their sensational effects, Wolf Messing did not. As the story goes, the Soviet leader Joseph Stalin asked to see the psychic. He told his head of security to get the message to Messing that he was to be in Stalin's office at the Kremlin within three days. He also told the security chief not to give the man a pass; if he was as good as he claimed, he should be able to get into the office without any passes, sanctions, or written material of any sort—even if it was the most closely guarded area in all the world.

Two days after the request was made, Stalin looked up from his desk to see a man standing in front of him. Not only was this a breach of security, but to his mind it was impossible. Calling out for his security people, he pressed hidden buttons that rang loud clanging bells and alarms. The entire floor was soon in an uproar. Guards ran in and surrounded the stranger. When the man was questioned, he revealed himself to be Wolf Messing, simply complying with Stalin's request for an appearance.

On further questioning as to how he accomplished it, he said that he laid a cloak of invisibility over himself by saying the words, "Beria, Beria, I am Beria," and repeating it until he believed it himself. When questioned, the guards said that the only person who'd passed them was the head of the Soviet secret police, their chief of security, Lavrenti Beria.

Wolf Messing's feat is a remarkable demonstration of the concept of power words. Examples of the use of power words are all around us, from the shouts of martial arts practitioners to the "fore!" of golfers. Despite the prevalence and obvious utility of this concept, however, it seldom occurs to most people to apply it in their own lives. In this chapter we'll give a more complete explanation of its use and range of applications so that you can add another valuable tool to your mental warehouse.

An example of the dynamic force of the words of power came from our own Silva research at Hallahan High School in Philadelphia, Pennsylvania.* A teenage girl feared some of the local toughs in the school after suffering several verbal assaults by them in the past. The team of Silva instructors went through our modified program with the students, after which other Silva people conducted follow-up research. The stu-

---

* De Sau, George, "Hallahan High Pre- and Post-Testing" (Laredo, Tex.: Silva Mind Control International Inc., 1973).

dents who participated, it was found, gained different resources from the program depending on their individual problems.

The girl in question was particularly interested in the concept of power words. Her main interest was in keeping herself safe from harm, and she felt that learning power words would accomplish the most good. The day after the team left, she subsequently reported, she was walking into the school yard past the group she feared, and instead of expecting sneers, smirks, someone tripping her, or perhaps a punch on the arm or worse, she concentrated on the power word *beware*.

She repeated the word *beware* over and over again mentally as she had been taught. Putting her three fingers together to trigger the technique, she visualized a quiet *beware* in her mind growing louder and louder until the word filled her consciousness. Approaching the group with her head held high and concentrating on the word *beware,* she strolled right on past the group, and for the first time she could remember, not one of them said or did anything to harm her in the slightest. Indeed, she said, they acted as though she wasn't even there.

Reasons abound for the effectiveness of the power word. There is the expectation that things will be right. There is the elimination of the negative expectation of fear, thereby producing a stress-free and relaxed state of mind. And not the least, there is the faith that the word instills in an individual. Here's how to use the concept of power words as a resource to help better your life.

Begin with a simple word, one that will demonstrate to you the effectiveness of the power word concept. The first power word for you to use is the word *power* itself. You may use the three-finger technique by placing the first three fingers of either hand together as a trigger device to enhance its use.

Think the word *power* for thirty seconds, repeating the word every two or three seconds. Begin with a diminished image in a small white frame and then enhance the image by enlarging the frame. Enlarge the word so that you can see it in huge letters on the side of a mountain. At the same time, hear the word spoken, becoming louder and louder. Mentally shout out the word *power,* feeling yourself become more powerful as you do. Take a few steps as you do this and you will notice that you are walking taller, straighter, and with more confidence. You may be able to feel new strength surging through your body.

That is the concept and use of the power word.

During the Silva Mental Dynamics seminar we demonstrate the action of the power word. Each person sitting in the front row of seats is given a word to repeat mentally. The instructor whispers to half of them to think *strong;* the other half, to think *weak.* All are told to hold their right arms straight out and away from their bodies. The instructor then strolls by and attempts to pull down each arm.

What follows is a gasp of astonishment and amusement from the students in the seminar as they realize that something unusual has taken place. Half of the front-row occupants end up with an arm down, while the rest stand with arms straight out and rigid. All those who were told to repeat the power word *strong* have their right arms extended; the instructor could not pull them down. The rest stand looking somewhat sheepish, with their right arms loosely dangling at their sides. The power words used have weakened those who thought *weak* and strengthened those who thought *strong*.

A strong, healthy bull of a man, believing that for some reason he is weak due to an imagined problem, or that someone he is going to meet is stronger than he, will in fact be weakened. This has been proven many times in the professional arenas of the world, especially with boxers who attempt to "spook" or weaken their opponents with words of power for themselves and weakness for their opponent.

The same effect is seen in the home-team advantage that has been well documented over the years in every high school, college, and professional stadium in the world. When you get thousands of people together thinking of their man, woman, or team winning, those thoughts generate a feeling of power in the team members. The home-team advantage is enhanced even more when all the spectators use the same word, as they do when chanting the name of a favorite player.

You can use the technique of power words to create an immediate change in your actions. Whether it involves a change from cowardice to courage, procrastination to motivation, or lethargy to activity, there is a word for you. Say that you wish to do something now that you have been putting off. Create a mental image of yourself doing this thing. You can add to the technique by brightening the image and then enlarging and zooming in on it. Once you have a clear image in your mind, repeat the appropriate power word, in this case *energize*. Repeat the word over and over while holding the image of the thing you wish to do.

EMPOWERMENT

You will find your energy building to the stage where you will in fact energize yourself to do it.

There are many words that you can use as power words. *Strength, health, beware, handsome, beautiful, strong, powerful, courageous, fearless, thin, relaxed, successful, effective, attract, repel, creative,* are but a handful. See how many more you can think of that would be useful to you.

When you understand that you are in control, and that one of the tools of that control is the directed use of the power word, then you can change, by degrees, from weak to strong, from fearful to courageous, from fat to thin, from putting things off to getting them done, and from failure to success in any goal you direct the powerful force of your mind to achieve.

Chapter 16

WEIGHT CONTROL

Take a trip to your local book shop and examine the weight control section. You will find just about anything that you are looking for. Want a diet where meat eating predominates? It's there. You don't care for meat and want a vegetarian diet? It's there. Like to drink alcoholic beverages? There is a drinking person's diet. Don't care for water? There is a reduced-liquid diet. Enjoy water? There is a water diet. You will find a fruit diet, a juice diet, a cheese diet, an egg diet, a rice diet, a bread diet, a high-protein diet, a low-protein diet, a low-cholesterol diet, a high-cholesterol diet, a fat-free diet and a fat diet, a low-salt diet and a high-salt diet, a yogurt diet, a low-fiber diet and a high-fiber diet, and if you were to accept the breatharian philosophy, a food-free air diet.

Most of these diet books were written by medical authorities, doctors and nutritionists, and most of them contradict one another.

Whom are we to believe? What are we to believe?

Let us analyze an overweight individual. Except in rare cases, an excessive intake of food results in the body storing the calories it does not use for kinetic energy (energy in motion) as potential energy (energy awaiting use) in the form of body fat, resulting in an overweight condition. In other words, people who are overweight eat too much.

The solution is simple, and obvious. No magic about it, and everyone knows the answer. It can be stated in two words: *eat less*.

How easy.

How difficult!

Let's explore the difficulty; for there are many insidious forces at work here.

First off, we will examine the body's viewpoint with respect to food. Whatever it is within the body that defines that hollow feeling in the stomach as a need for food is one of the basic problems. Since analogies and metaphors often bring answers in an abstract form that leads to a clearer understanding, let's construct one now.

There are two basic types of energy, potential and kinetic. Potential energy is energy contained and awaiting use. Kinetic energy is energy in motion.

Say that you have an old-fashioned watch with a mainspring. You tighten the spring by inserting a key in the proper place on the watch and turning it to coil the watch spring tightly. A transference of energy takes place. You transfer the energy of your fingers to the key, to the gears, to the mainspring, where the energy is stored. As the spring slowly uncoils the energy becomes kinetic, causing the hands to move so that you can tell the time.

Once you have turned the key so that the spring is fully wound, it would be difficult to turn it any more. Imagine what would happen to the watch if you were to take a pair of pliers and, using all of your strength, turn the key again, and then again, and then once more.

Your timepiece would ultimately burst into a mass of screws, wire, and metal bits as the overwound mainspring, which cannot contain all the energy forced into it, finally flies all over the place. Overwinding was the main cause of broken watches in the early part of the century before tiny clutches were devised to take the pressure off the gear system and make overwinding impossible.

Now let us see how that metaphor applies to people.

Food is potential energy. You use this energy (turn it kinetic) when you walk, when you talk, when you think, when you eat. You even use a portion of it lying in bed staring at the ceiling. You might say that the equivalent to winding a watch would be feeding yourself.

It takes much less food than is generally thought to produce the energy that most people need. Intellectually, most people know that after a good breakfast and before a substantial dinner, an apple or any other piece of fruit would make for a wholesome light lunch. Then why overwind the watch? Why consume a lunch that would adequately feed some people for two days? Certainly not for the food value. What then?

Here are only a few of the reasons that people overeat: *Guilt. Socializing. Substitution. Purposeful distortion of the way they look. Need for love.*

Guilt: There are those people who feel that because so many people can't afford even the basic sustenance to keep their children alive, it would be a sin not to eat every bite of food placed in front of them. Then they eat far past the point of satisfying hunger. There are also those who feel that the richer (and fattening) foods are expensive, and by leaving any provisions on the plate, they are throwing away money.

Socializing: "Let's talk about it over doughnuts and coffee." "We'll go over that at lunch." "I'll meet you for dinner." "Let's discuss that over a drink." "Two Seasons has the greatest margaritas in town; let's go over the terms there." "I've discovered the greatest pie shop, let's talk when we get there." And on and on. It sometimes comes as a great revelation when people discover that they can socialize without putting something in their mouths.

Substitution: Gorging oneself, having that extra helping, choosing that extra big cut, is often a substitution for something you want and do not have. Gluttony is an acceptable vice and the easiest vice to satisfy, and so the normal transferral of one need to another is by way of food.

Purposeful distortion: In a recent Silva class a grossly overweight woman stood up and asked why she could not stop overeating, why she sneaked extra portions and sometimes ate four full meals a day. With tears in her eyes and a catch in her voice, she said, "People always tell me not to eat so much. But they never tell me how. How do I stop?"

Looking at the sad woman and sensing the answer she needed was more than just that of telling her to diet or exercise—she already knew that—the instructor felt an inspired need to ask her point-blank, "Does your husband still love you?" This seemed to have nothing at all to do with her question and startled her for a moment.

She stood there, leaning on the chair in front of her, blinking for a long moment, and then tears rolled down her eyes as she shook her head and said with a half sigh, "I don't know."

Actually she hated herself because she disliked intensely the reflection of that self she saw in the mirror. She knew herself better than anyone else did. If, knowing herself as well as she did, she hated herself, how could anyone else not dislike her? With a philosophy like that it would be difficult for her to believe that anyone could even like, much less love her.

She believed that her husband didn't love her because of the way she looked. "Well," she subconsciously thought, "that's all right. I don't love the way I look either, so why should my husband?" She could cope with that.

But if she were to lose weight, look good, and come to like herself again, and her husband still did not love her, then it was *her* he didn't love, and not the way she looked. And that she couldn't cope with.

No matter how many diets she went on, there was no way that her inner consciousness was going to allow her to lose weight and look good. Looking good was seen as a threat by her inner consciousness and was to be avoided at any and all costs.

Need for love: Many people heard words like these when they were children: "Eat everything on your plate, dear" or "If you want Mommy to love you, you'd better eat those peas." Or spinach, or squash, or whatever.

Hearing this over a period of time, the child soon equates food with love. As an adult needing love, he or she eats because food equals love. If you can't find love, find food; eat it all up, every bit; isn't that when Mommy loves you the most?

Lack of love, moreover, feels like an emptiness. Many who want to fill that emptiness with love fill up with food instead.

With so many reasons for eating and overeating, it's a wonder that everyone isn't overweight. Why aren't they? As with all things, one's viewpoint is critical. Food represents different things to different people.

Do you see food as a means of socializing, as a substitute, as a method of keeping your self-esteem, or as an expression of love? Or do you see food as energy, pure and simple, like a log on the fire, gasoline for the car, or electricity for your lights? If you're overweight, you can bet that you don't view food as energy, and that your problem is covered in one of the above groups.

Many people have gone on ten-day fasts and felt the better for it. A few people have gone on forty-day fasts. Therefore we must assume that the average, healthy body can get along just fine without food for, let's say conservatively, five days. And yet there are people who can eat two eggs, potatoes, toast, and coffee at 8:00 A.M., a danish pastry and coffee at 10:30 A.M., and then at 1:00 P.M. say, "I'm starving, let's get a bite of lunch."

Obviously, you can't "starve" between breakfast and lunch, so what is the reason for the hunger pangs?

The answer is semantic. The empty stomach message you are receiving is only being interpreted as hunger pangs. What it really is, is potential energy wanting to turn kinetic. This feeling of energy has been interpreted as hunger for so long that it has become an empty stomach feeling, when actually your body is telling you that it has energy to spare, please put it to some use. But instead of using it in play, or exercise, or work, the energy is used in eating. The body has plenty of fuel and is demanding use with the message, but instead more fuel is thrown into the stomach and the energy turns inward to digest the new onslaught of food that the body didn't want in the first place. After eating, the feeling of energy turns into a feeling of lethargy as the kinetic energy builds still more of a potential reserve.

Learn to interpret this feeling of hunger as energy. Then use the energy. You will soon find that you have more energy than you've had since you were a teenager and before you learned to interpret the energy message as a feeling of hunger.

In the beginning of this chapter you read that there was no magic to reducing your weight; all you had to do was to eat less. That's the greatest diet in the world. An even better diet can be summed up in four words. "Eat less; exercise more." And that is really all there is to it.

Here is one excellent way to eat less. It may pose a problem if you have a guilt complex, but that will clear up once the pattern of eating less is established. Order what you normally do when dining at a restaurant and serve your usual portions when dining at home, but eat only half of what's on your plate. Before you begin eating, divide the portions in half and eat only half. It is a simple, uncomplicated method of eating less.

Eat fruit. For more than a hundred years, indeed

159

since the first book on diets was written late in the last century, dietitians have recommended fruit consumption as one meal of the day. By eating an orange or two, or an apple and a banana, you will find that your hunger message disappears, and you will still have the energy to put to some use. A full diet of fruit is not recommended, since we need more nutrients than a fruit regimen can provide.

Once you get used to eating a few pieces of fruit for breakfast, lunch, or dinner, you will find many of your eating habits changing. You really do not need a formal diet. We do not recommend any of them because all of them tend to control you, and since no one enjoys being controlled by an outside force, you will be subconsciously fighting any diet.

Better to modify your diet; that you can do. It is much easier, for example, to eliminate a type of food that you believe may be causing you a problem—sugar perhaps. Simply eliminate sugar and you will be well on the way to recovery. You know which foods are heavily sugared: cake, cookies, candy, ice cream, desserts, and so forth. You cannot avoid sugar totally; it is in almost all processed foods and in most breads. It's not necessary to eliminate it, though, only modify your intake.

You may decide to eliminate bread from your eating program, or salad dressings, or oil and butter, or alcohol. You may decide simply to modify your eating habits by eating moderately and enjoying it more.

In Chapter 3, "Five Rules of Happiness," you learned that the first rule is "If you like a thing, enjoy it," and that the two emotions that prevent a person from enjoyment are fear and guilt. With respect to food, both of these emotions come into play.

One person who attended the Silva Mental Dynamics weekend seminar had a problem with both fear and guilt and his downfall was apple pie with a large slab of vanilla ice cream on top of it. The man was overweight and always on one diet or another, but he could not bring himself to give up the pie and ice cream. He sneaked out of the house to the local restaurant and crammed the dessert down his throat every day, looking about him furtively for anyone he knew who might see him there, feeling guilty about the entire process. He was afraid of the consequences of what he was doing, and for hours afterward asked himself why he did it. Then the longing and inordinate desire overwhelmed him once again and he looked for a means to sneak out of the house so that he could gorge on apple pie and ice cream once more.

After the seminar he decided that if he was going to eat the pie, he was going to enjoy it. One of the keys to satisfaction is moderation. When you are moderate in the things that you do, you are generally happy about the outcome. And so our overweight friend decided that he would be moderate. He would set a day for himself that would be apple-pie-and-ice-cream day and on that day he would eat without fear and without guilt. He decided that once a week would do it for him. As long as he knew that on each Tuesday he could have his pie and ice cream, he could live his life during the rest of the week without the incessant craving. He programmed himself to that degree at level and lo and behold, it worked.

When the day came, he enjoyed his pie and ice cream as he never had before. It was, as he reported, a miracle. After four weeks he changed the schedule to monthly pie-and-ice-cream days. After three more months, when pie and ice cream day came around, he didn't feel like any and so did not have any. He reported to the people at a subsequent seminar that for the first time in as long as he could remember he felt truly free and in control.

And yes, he did reduce his weight to where he wanted to be and has kept to his present size. Without dieting. Simply by eating the same foods he had always eaten, but in moderation. Of course all that extra energy he had caused him to think about putting it to some use, and so he started taking long walks to use the energy, and that beneficial side effect helped in his reduction program as well.

How to lose weight:

1. Accept the fact that you are overweight. Admit it if you are.

2. Have a strong desire to rid yourself of weight.

3. Go to level and see if any of the reasons cited in this chapter applies to you.

4. Learn to interpret the hunger pangs you feel four or five hours after eating as potential energy waiting to turn kinetic.

5. Learn the approximate caloric values of the food that you eat, and substitute a low-calorie item for a high-calorie one whenever possible.

6. Modify your food intake.

7. Eat less, exercise more.

Chapter 17

ASSERTIVENESS AND UNVICTIMIZATION

Many law enforcement experts feel that there are people who have a "victim's personality." These people seem to attract aggressors somehow. It's as though they were sending out some kind of a message, the way a flower sends a message to attract a bee, except instead of an odor, it's a vibration. When this vibration enters the field of an aggressor, it causes an attraction and victim and aggressor come together in an episode of some sort. There are those who are constantly having problems: burglaries, assaults, robberies, rude and abusive treatment, and negative experiences in general. Victims.

Do you have a victim's personality? Let's see.

Have you ever gone into a restaurant and been led to a table next to a swinging toilet door, or a busy coffee station, or a person smoking a cigar, or a screaming baby? You take the seat and grumble something like, "There it is again; it always happens to me." Or, have you ever bought something in a department store only to be given your purchase in a crushed box that you do not like? You take the box and shake your head, thinking, "I always seem to get the second-rate stuff."

If similar things happen to you, then you could be well on the way to developing a victim's personality, if indeed you do not already have one. But how does one get rid of a victim's personality? Is it possible?

Yes, it is. By using the principle of correspondence (as above so below, as below so above), we unlock the entire chain of victimization. In other words, we work on the low end to unlock the high. We work on the minor to effect the major. Generally a person who is victimized in a minor way is the same person who is victimized in a major way in life. And the personality who accepts the unwanted seat at the restaurant is the same type of person who gets his or her house robbed. If we can end victimization in the simpler arenas, we're well on the way to ending it in the more complex.

How, then, to unvictimize oneself? Say you go into a restaurant and you're given a table you don't like. You call the host or hostess over and say, "I do not like this table. Please give me another." Chances are in most instances, you will get a better table. You are no longer a victim.

You go to a department store and purchase something that comes in a crushed box. You state, "I don't like this box, it's damaged." In all probability you will receive another box.

But what if you don't get another table or a new box? You're still not a victim. You have asserted yourself. You have taken action rather than passively accepting. You've asked for a better table, a new box, and in so doing *you have set yourself up for choice.*

Now *you* have a choice. You can stay in the restaurant or leave, but the choice is yours, not someone else's. You have a choice in the department store; you can accept the box, or reject it, but the choice is yours.

To be a bit more assertive, you might say something like, "Let me speak to your superior" and go on to the next echelon of sales personnel. Wonderful words those, "Let me speak to your superior." Almost invariably, you will be able to speak with the person's immediate superior, and generally, if your cause is sound, you will get satisfaction.

Once you turn the tables to allow yourself a choice, you are no longer a victim. So the next time you're dissatisfied with anything, tell the person you're dealing with that you are dissatisfied and you'll find you are no longer a victim. You'll have taken the first step toward assertiveness.

People often ask what is the difference between assertiveness and aggressiveness. We would say that the difference is that assertiveness is done with kindness and a smile. Aggressiveness is the hand banging on the table, demanding satisfaction; we don't want any of that. When you make your request, do it courteously, and with a smile. Compliment when you can, but not excessively. Be moderate in all things.

After using these methods for a while you will find that it's fun. Life is a game, when you see it as such. Play the game. There's nothing to be angry or resentful about. When you realize that all people are operating in the same way—that is, from their own points of view—you begin to understand that everyone is right.

They are right because they believe they are right. But you are right as well. And the world starts with your viewpoint. When you realize that others too are right, for them, it becomes increasingly difficult to get angry at another person, especially if you have a strong self-image. You act a lot, but react less and less. Reactors are controlled by someone else; actors control themselves.

And that is one of the main differences between the timid victim and the assertive person. Knowing that you're right gives you the feeling of legitimacy that allows you to assert yourself. Knowing that others consider themselves right allows you to assert yourself without anger. And taking action when you feel victimized reinforces you as an actor, not reactor, so that passivity, resentment, and abuse will seldom be your lot.

Know that you deserve good treatment, act courteously to demand it, and it will usually be yours. If not from others in every instance, you'll know you can count on it from yourself.

Chapter 18

MOTIVATION AND PROCRASTINATION

There's a story about one James C. that speaks to us about motivation and procrastination.

"Jimmy the Gent," as he was known to friends, was the nicest guy you could ever hope to meet, but one of the worst procrastinators you'd ever run into. Jimmy would put off going to the bathroom until he was about ready to burst. He was late for his wedding, didn't get to the hospital until an hour after his daughter was born, and used to brag about having been to twelve Broadway plays without seeing the first fifteen minutes of any of them. Jimmy would put off putting something off if he could figure out a way to do it.

Jimmy worked his way into a reporter's spot on the *New York Post*. He was always late, but he was so good at what he did that the managing editor let him get away with it. One day a story broke and Jimmy, as usual, was the last one on the scene, which was an apartment house just off Second Avenue on Fifty-eighth Street. He got the same story all the other reporters got except he missed the fact that they all had to meet at the nearby station house for some fill-in information. Not getting the message because he wasn't there when it was handed out, Jimmy hung around the scene of the story.

After everyone else had left, Jimmy was standing around chewing on the tip of a pencil he was taking notes with when a woman ran out of the apartment house crying for the police, yelling that a burglar was stuck in a commode in her bathroom. This stirred up Jimmy's curiosity, and he went inside to check it out. Sure enough, when he got up to the woman's bathroom, there was a big mug hopping around on one foot with the other jammed into the bowl of the commode. It seems he was hiding in the john and when he heard the police coming up the stairs, he started flushing some drugs away. The stuff wasn't going down fast enough, so he stuck his foot in to help it along, and there he was, stuck. When Jimmy entered, the man offered him a hundred dollars to pull his foot out of the bowl.

Jimmy sat down on the edge of the bathtub to think this thing out. If he pulled the leg out, he figured, he'd be a hundred to the good. If he left the bozo's foot where it was, he might have some kind of story. What to do? While he was sitting there pondering this dilemma, the guy hopping around cursed a blue streak trying to motivate Jimmy to get off the bathtub and pull his foot out, but Jimmy didn't move.

With all the screaming and hollering, someone called the police and back they came, followed by all the reporters who were getting the information on the first problem. The man with his foot stuck in the bowl became agitated when he heard the sirens, grabbed his leg with both hands, and gave one last almighty tug. The whole toilet broke loose and he flew backward with his foot still stuck in the bowl. He fell on his back, his leg swung up over his head, and the commode whirled around and landed right on Jimmy the Gent's head, breaking into a hundred pieces. Jimmy was knocked out, and when he opened his eyes, it was two days later and he was lying in a midtown hospital bed with his head swathed in so many bandages he looked like a Bedouin.

When Jimmy tried to explain to his editor that he didn't turn in the story because he got kicked in the head with a toilet filled with dope, the man became excited and fired Jimmy. Apparently this wasn't the first credibility-stretching excuse Jimmy had brought back.

It was here that Silva Mental Dynamics entered the picture, because Jimmy came to the seminar strictly for the segment on procrastination. If anything good is to come out of this, he'd concluded, he had to become a man motivated. He promised himself two things: he'd keep his next job long enough to earn vacation time, and he'd see a musical from the first-act curtain for once.

After completing the class, he came to see that his problem was not having enough desire. With his new understanding of the cause of his procrastination, and his still painful headache from the boff he took, Jimmy determined to prove himself one motivated gent at his next job.

EMPOWERMENT

Eventually Jimmy landed a job in New Jersey on a small newspaper consisting mostly of ads and not much else. Jimmy was their only reporter. All they needed from him was some local gossip once a week. Jimmy's deadline for the news was three o'clock in the afternoon every Wednesday. No problem, except for the fact that the woman running the show required Jimmy to hand in a preliminary report on how the story was coming along on Tuesday morning at ten o'clock sharp. Two deadlines to meet. Two opportunities for procrastination.

But when Monday came, Jimmy had his story. It was all written in his head, which now looked like any other normal head since the bandages had come off a couple of days earlier. Unfortunately, inside his head is not what the boss wanted. Not being either clairvoyant or particularly indulgent of Jimmy's problem, she asked for the report to be written on a sheet of paper. Preferably typed, with correct spellings, so that she could read it.

This was Jimmy's seventh job in a year, and he was determined to keep it. So he sat down at his desk, put a sheet of paper in the typewriter, and thought about the story that he now had to pull out of his head and get on paper. But nothing happened. That story got stuck somewhere between Jimmy's left ear and the back of his right eye.

He let out a big sigh, closed his eyes, and thought back to the motivation part of the seminar he'd just gone through the week before.

He reviewed the seminar material on motivation and procrastination in hopes that he could now put an end to his lifelong habit.

Let's break into Jimmy's story at this point to

introduce the concepts that Jimmy was reviewing as he sat at his typewriter.

The principle of polarity states that all things have an opposite, and that opposites are basically the same thing, differing only by degree. Motivation and procrastination are examples of such opposites; they are essentially the same, both having to do with amount of desire to do something. And they differ as to the degree of desire involved.

If we were to imagine the polarization scale, on the negative end, the left end, we'd write the word *procrastination,* and under that write *weak desire.* At the opposite end of the yardstick, the positive side, we'd write the word *motivation,* and under that write *strong desire.*

When you have a strong desire to do something, then you are far over on the motivation side of the scale. As your desire weakens, you feel less and less motivated, until you enter the procrastination end of the scale. By the time your weakening desire reaches the end of the scale, you have no desire whatever to do the thing and so it never gets done.

Motivation very simply is strong desire. If your desire to do something is strong enough, you will do it. There are certain things that you need no motivation to do for they are subconscious and taken care of by your inner consciousness. You don't have to motivate yourself to breathe, for instance. Your body handles that very well all by itself. You don't have to motivate yourself to sleep, to drink, or to eat. You sleep when you're sleepy, you eat when you're hungry, you drink when you're thirsty. You breathe automatically whenever you require a breath.

But take away any one of these necessities and your desire to get it back would be so strong that you would be motivated instantly to succeed. You'd do anything for breath. If someone were choking you so that you couldn't breathe, you would be so motivated to breathe that you would kill that person to get that person's hands from your neck. Go without water for two or three days and you would be so motivated by your desire for water that you would break through walls to get to water.

What is it that you wish to motivate yourself to do? What have you been putting off that you'd really like to accomplish? Go to your Alpha level and consider the question. Once you have come up with an action you'd like to motivate yourself to do, think about your feelings toward it. Do you have a strong desire for the positive outcome? If you have been procrastinating, it is due to a weak desire. The answer, then, is to build desire. How do you build your desire?

Say that at one end of the scale you have a weak desire, a desire perhaps for a sip of water. You're sitting comfortably in a chair, reading a book, watching television, or looking over the newspaper, and you want a drink of water. You think about how nice it would be but you're just not thirsty enough to get up and so you continue reading. That's weak desire. You are on the negative end, the procrastination end, of the scale. You will put off getting that drink of water. The only way to motivate yourself to get up and get the drink of water is to build a stronger desire for it in your mind.

The way to build stronger desire is to work with an image of the thing desired. In the case of fetching a glass of water, you'd go to level and visualize an image of the glass of cool, refreshing water. You'd see yourself putting the glass to your lips and feel the water trickling down your throat, satisfying you. You'd enhance the visualization through the Golden Image technique, and soon your desire would build and you'd get up and satisfy your thirst.

The process is the same with any action you want to motivate yourself to accomplish.

Now consider what you have chosen to enhance your desire for. Consider all aspects of this goal. First, ask yourself why do you wish to do this? If you do it successfully, what will be the result? What are you going to do when this goal is accomplished? Visualize your circumstances after the goal is achieved.

Next, imagine doing the thing you've been putting off. Picture yourself actually doing it. Now make three decisions. First, decide when you're going to do it. Set a definite, realistic date. Second, decide where you're going to do it. And third, decide how you're going to go about it. How will you begin it? How will you sustain it, bring it to maturity? While you're considering when, where, and how, visualize yourself going about doing these actions.

Now that you've decided when you're going to start, where you're going to start it, and how you're going to start and go about it, and you know why you're going to do it, the only thing remaining is to build your desire through a visual image. And let us now address visualization or imagery as a means of enhancing desire and motivation.

Visualization is a key part of a process that leads to action. This process starts with thought, leads to a buildup of energy, and results in action. The function of visualization is to generate the energy buildup that leads to action or activity.

Uncontrolled, this trio of thought, energy buildup, and action can be manifested as an unhealthy obsession. Obsessive people concentrate on one thing to the exclusion of all others; their thought processes exclude all outside interference. They're so focused on the object of the obsession that their energy builds to an enormous degree, becoming so overwhelming that they do not think of the consequences of their actions.

On the other hand, a *controlled* buildup of energy through a concentration of thought accompanied by a visual image can be positive and motivating. And this is our goal: to control the ultimate action of the buildup of energy by controlling the thought and thereby influencing the energy buildup and subsequent action, through the power of visualization.

To stimulate this energy, go to level and concentrate on the action you want to bring about. By focusing your attention on the image of yourself accomplishing the goal, you build this energy for the ultimate action. And the more you concentrate on the image, the more you build desire. By concentrating on the image daily, you'll find your desire growing stronger and stronger until the energy buildup will be irresistible and you will have motivated yourself to do what you previously put off.

And now, having dissected motivation and procrastination and suggested ways to deal with them, we'll return to the story of Jimmy the Gent.

All the thoughts and concepts he'd learned in the Silva seminar went through the mind of Mr. James C.

as he sat at his desk trying to motivate himself to write out his report. There were a number of key points he wrote down as they came to mind.

"One, I have to strengthen my desire to write this preliminary report on the story. Two, I've got to enhance my visualization. Three, I must picture the positive result of the report. Four, I've got to think about exactly when I am going to start, where I'm going to do it, and how I'll go about doing it. Five, I'll concentrate on the visual image of successfully finishing the report to generate a buildup of energy.

"Let's see now. I enhance my desire by thinking about the thing."

Jimmy closed his eyes and concentrated on the report itself. He visualized it finished and on his desk, neatly typed. He saw himself smiling and satisfied.

"Okay, I've done that. Now I have to strengthen the visualization."

Next, he made the picture brighter. After he brightened the visualization, he made it more colorful. Sitting at his desk with his eyes closed, he next made the visualization clearer and three-dimensional. Then he made it larger. He was entirely involved with the report now. It was the only thing that he was conscious of.

His next thought was, "What will the positive result of this report be?"

Still with eyes closed, he saw his employer reading the report and nodding, a smile of satisfaction on her face. He visualized her telling him of a job well done. He saw her at a later date giving him a raise, promoting him. A smile broke out on Jimmy's face as his next thought came to mind.

"When do I start?" he thought as the visual image

of him writing the report came. He mentally noted the starting time on the clock; it indicated 11:35 A.M. "Where? That's easy—here at this desk.

"How am I going to start? That's easy too. I'm just going to turn on the typewriter and start pecking away."

Jimmy saw himself typing and enhanced that image. Finally he thought about what visual image might build up the energy that could carry him from thought to action.

At this point he visualized himself on a beach in Nassau, his favorite place in the Bahamas. It had been several years since he'd accumulated enough vacation time to be able to go there. He sighed gently as his head bobbed up and down. "Sure enough, that's why I'm doing this. I want to lie around in the warm sun for a while, and this is a sure way to get there, through my work."

Finally Jimmy opened his eyes and looked at the clock on the wall. It read ten-fifty. Jimmy thought, "Ah, the hell with it, I'm going to start anyhow." And he began to type furiously. It was still early but Jimmy was no longer involved with the time of day; instead he was swept up in action of the present. And now was when he was going to complete his preliminary report. After that he might just go on and finish off his story. What the heck, he had plenty of time, might as well put it to good use.

Chapter 19

ENHANCING SENSUAL DESIRE

People are products of their desires. Whatever you desire with sufficient strength you will probably attain. When breath is denied, the desire to breathe is so strong that all else shrinks to insignificance. No one has to tell you to build a golden or any other image when that happens; the image is there instantly and will remain until a breath is taken. No one needs instruction on enhancing the breath of life, the ultimate desire.

In Chapter 18 we discussed the way increasing desire strengthens your motivation. The lessons of that discussion are useful when it comes to the desire for achievement, for success, for ridding yourself of a problem, and countless other areas in your life. But what of other desires? What of the sensual desires? What about the desire to enhance a flagging sexual drive, to stimulate a waning interest in food, to reawaken the wonder at the beauty of nature, or to create beauty from a stark gray canvas?

EMPOWERMENT

It has been said that true education is telling people what they already know, in different terms, for greater understanding. If you have studied the Golden Image concept, then you already know the answers. But let's delve a bit deeper. What follows is an explanation of the use of the Golden Image to enhance desire.

One of the most common problems people have with weak sensual desire is in the area of sex. When you harbor any fears about sex, it brings stress into the experience, and your relaxation fades or disappears. The mental pictures you create will be colored by that fear, and your expectations of a negative occurrence will diminish or destroy your desire.

When neither partner brings fears or problems from previous experiences into the present experience, both are free of negative imagery, relaxed and comfortable, and better equipped both physically and mentally to merge and become as one. The relaxed state of mind produces imagery of ideal feminine-masculine characteristics and the perfect union takes place.

Both the male and the female bodies are constructed to react to this imagery. The male reacts to the chemicals flowing through his body with strength and vitality. A portion of that vitality causes changes in the body that can be neutralized by negative imagery, causing a stilted performance at best and impotence at worst.

The female reacts to the chemicals flowing through her body with mucus production and relaxed receptivity as she readies for the experience. The slightest degree of stress caused by a negative attitude, guilt, or fear will bring about the opposite result—

constriction, dryness, and muscular tension creating difficulty if not pain.

Stress is not the only cause of problems with sexual desire. One of the problems commonly encountered by couples who have been familiar for a long period of time is not so much that there are no longer any surprises, and not so much that familiarity tends to breed boredom, but rather that the mental pictures preceding the action have become automatic, and tend to gray out and diminish. When they were fresh and new, they were golden—brighter and more colorful, more vivid. The old mental imagery is like a familiar flowering bush in your backyard. It's lovely and fragrant, but you've seen it so many times you walk right on by without taking any notice.

If you were to close your eyes and imagine doing things with that bush that you had never done or imagined before, you would see it from a different perspective. Say that you were to imagine yourself taking the bush out and planting it in the middle of your living room. Or see yourself driving with the bush in your car, giving it a bath, pruning it, digging around the base and raking in nutriments. Imagine it growing larger, getting smaller, changing in color. Suddenly you notice your beautiful flowering bush. You have restored your interest in it.

Sex and desire are primarily mental functions, and an understanding of the Golden Image will certainly help to reinvigorate desire. Think about a time when you had a sensational sexual experience. Now make the visualization of that experience brighter. Make it bigger and focus in on a portion of the scene. Make it three-dimensional, give it depth. Bring your sense of touch, feel with your fingers, your lips, your body, your skin. Bring in sound. What did your body feel like? What were your emotions? Enhance the feelings.

Now view the scene as though it were being acted at a theater. You are sitting in third row center and can see yourself as a player involved in all the activity. Walk onto the stage and examine the action at closer range. When you find a portion of the scene that attracts you, slow time down and see the activity in slow motion. When you come to a part of the scene that is of greatest attraction, jump in and become active yourself. Become the action.

The next time you have a sexual experience use the same technique. About ten minutes or so before the activity, involve yourself in a recent similar experience and develop a Golden Image of that experience. Then switch your viewpoint to the present and create a Golden Image for what you are about to experience.

To enhance your desire for a different type of activity you do the same thing. You visualize a recent similar, successful time, and create a Golden Image of it. Then you consider the experience that you are about to have. Think of all the positive aspects and enhance them. White-frame them, build on them, make them three-dimensional, enlarge the scene, make it vivid. Then experience it.

Do you want to stimulate an appetite for a food? Think of the last time you had that food and there was a particularly pleasant experience attached to it. Before you eat the food, visualize that pleasure. See yourself enjoying every mouthful. Bring in as many vivid, enhanced images as you can. Delight in it and your desire will grow.

By learning how to control desire you have added

one more resource to your mental bag of tricks. But what about diminishing desire? There will be times when you will want to lessen your desire for some reason. According to the principle of polarity, if you know how to enhance desire, you automatically know how to diminish it. You simply reverse the technique.

To diminish desire you blue-frame it. Allow the mental pictures to appear and then see them in black-and-white, smaller, drab and one-dimensional, smaller still until the image is so small that it has nearly disappeared. Then switch it with a white-framed and larger image. (See Chapter 5, "Golden Images," for a complete explanation.)

Sometimes it helps to bring in a contradictory image.

Say that you have a strong desire for the opposite sex and you'd like to diminish it for whatever reason. You have tried blue-framing the image and it didn't work. Try this: leave the image alone but bring in a troupe of clowns doing backflips behind the scene. See one of them squirting seltzer on the person in your image. Bring in a banjo player, a whole orchestra of banjo players. See Mickey Mouse playing a bagpipe; hear the bagpipe. There in a corner is a merry-go-round; hear the music. Where is your desire now?

This technique can be helpful if you're trying to fall out of love. Think about the person you continue to love too much. Get a good view of that person. See the person smiling at you. Put a clown hat and a red clown nose on the person and blacken two of the front teeth. Now bring in the orchestra of banjo players, the carousel, and the rest of the circus. Notice the change?

Among our great gifts are the senses that we have been supplied with by the Creator. We have five of them at our disposal—sight, hearing, smell, taste, and touch. Many people use their senses in much the same way as beginners use a computer—after hearing the commercials and purchasing a computer, they discover to their dismay that it takes a great deal of work to learn even the basics of the machine, and either relegate it to the closet or end up making use of a small percentage of its capabilities. Then there are those who learn the language of the computer, spend time and effort, and gain full benefit from the machine.

It is much the same with the senses. We have them and generally put them to use unconsciously. But every now and again a Michelangelo comes along whose senses are the same but have been honed to such a degree that he can look at a ten-foot-square, solid block of marble and see a figure trapped inside. It takes only a hammer and chisel to release the figure. Now that is an extraordinary use of the sense of sight.

What of a Vincent Van Gogh, who could look at a flower, seeing what only he could see, and paint such a representation of that flower that a hundred years later the painting would evoke a sensory cascade of all the flowers that have ever been? Or a Ray Charles, who could take a musical note and stretch it with his voice into such a thing of beauty that even detractors would swell with the sensual perfection of the sound?

When we hear the term *gifted people,* we generally think about those who have in some manner perfected one or more of those five senses. Do they have a different set of senses? A larger brain? A greater capacity for utilizing information? No. They simply make better use of what they have.

It is now time for a lesson in the use of the senses.

To enhance the desire to see things more clearly and in greater depth, we will use the technique of the Golden Image. Let's begin with a blank sheet of white paper. Get a pencil or pen and a sheet of paper. Draw a circle on the paper about the size of a coffee-cup lid. Stare at the circle for a moment and then close your eyes and mentally pick the circle up to look under it, making it three-dimensional. The circle may turn into an umbrella with a person holding it. It may turn into an automobile tire, an AWACS jet, the roof of the Astrodome, or . . . what?

Next, look about you. What do you see? A couch, a book, a painting? Let's use a painting, or a picture of something. If there is not one within view, find one.

Look at the picture and then close your eyes and visualize what you have seen. If you need another look, open your eyes and then close them again. Go to level. Now imagine that you are in the painting and then look about you. What do you see? What do you sense?

Create a different background. Let your imagination run free. Bring anything you like into the painting. It will suddenly open into new vistas. Bring in new colors, scenery, vegetation, weather, sounds. Use your mighty imagination. After a few minutes of this, come out of level and once again look at the picture. See all the things you missed the first time. You will, in all probability, never again look at the picture the way you did before.

Let's turn to sound. Get a good cassette tape or record of a symphony or concerto written by a genius composer and played by an excellent orchestra under the baton of a gifted conductor. Play the cassette as you normally would. You may enjoy the music and you may not, but even if you are not inclined to classical music, listen anyway.

You will now develop your sense of hearing by listening for things you have not previously heard.

Play the tape once again. As it begins, take yourself to your Alpha level and listen to the music. Listen for the different sound qualities. Hear the intensity of the violins, the rich brassy blare of horns, the mellow warmth of basses, the twinkling cascade of the piano if there is one, the booming thunder of the drums. Pick out different lines of music to follow—the low bass instruments, the middle section, the highest voices in the orchestra. Notice how the composer introduces a melody, develops it, leaves it, and comes back to it in a new approach. Now feel yourself merge with the music. Imagine that you are music, that you are riding up and down with the melody. Feel every cell in your body responding to the vibrations of sound. What does the music tell you? Let the music take you to another time, another place. Imagine that you are somewhere else, somewhere the voice of the orchestra has led you. Enhance the scene. Bring in color, and wind, and the sea, and mountains; use your imagination.

When you come out of level, you will find that you have heard more than the ordinary listener hears. If you were lucky, you may have even heard what the composer intended when the piece was written.

To enhance touch, take a good look at a tree in your yard, on the street, or in a nearby park. Now put the first three fingers of either hand together, take a deep breath, and as you slowly exhale, mentally say the word *relax*. Look again at the tree. Imagine reaching out with a hand and feeling the surface of the tree. Move the mental hand gently up the tree, feeling each branch, each leaf. Reach down to the root system and feel the depth of the roots. Do it with love so that the tree will sense positive and satisfying things. Now move your mental hand into the tree. Get the sensation of the sap, and the life within the tree. Get an impression of the voice of the tree, the way that it sings when caressed by a breeze. Never again will you see that tree the way that you did before.

Look around you. Reach out with your mental hand and feel the ceiling. Note the texture. Now the carpet. The wall. A book. Whatever else is in the room. You do feel a difference, do you not? And yet, you are touching with your mind only.

Perhaps now you will understand the statement that Michelangelo made when asked about his carving ability. "It's nothing" was his response. "I see the figure in the block of marble and chip away the excess material."

As you become more familiar with these techniques, you will discover that you have more control over your desires. Practice and soon you will be able to enhance, or diminish, any desire of the senses that you wish to control.

PART FIVE

Improving Relationships

Chapter 20

RELATIONSHIP AWARENESS

To understand what a relationship is, how to bring one about, how to enhance one, and why relationships are diminished and lost, one must understand the force of need.

The most important thing in the world to us is our needs. They affect our opinions, our attitudes, and our viewpoint. Generally we're more aware of unfulfilled needs than the ones that are consistently met. Fundamental life needs in particular are so commonly accepted that we usually overlook them. No one is aware of the air breathed, the ground walked on, the water drunk, and yet these are the needs we miss most when gone. When we are deprived of any of the important basics in life, we suddenly see them more clearly and as through a magnifying glass, greatly enlarged.

There are other needs besides the basics, of course, and they multiply as we grow. An infant has needs similar to those of an adult: food, water, warmth, security, and someone seeing the good in them, or love. As we mature, the food, water, and warmth are often taken for granted, the needs being constantly supplied (for most of us). The basic needs are forgotten as other needs appear: a need for love, for sexual fulfillment, and for procreation; and that great one, the need for a sense of self-esteem. A need for liking who you are. Most of these needs, you will note, are emotional.

Then there are the needs for things, for activities: money is a need; work, vocations, avocations, and vacations are all needs.

The key to a good relationship is simple once you understand the role that needs play in making a relationship weak, moderate, average, or strong. Let's give the word *relationship* a different definition from the dictionary's, for unlocking the meaning of the word often leads to greater understanding.

Here is the word defined: *A good relationship is a mutual filling of needs.*

When two people have strong needs and each fills the other's needs, there is a powerful relationship. When two people have weak needs and each fills the other's needs, there is a mild relationship.

When either person has strong needs and those needs are not being filled, there is a poor relationship. When either has weak needs and those needs are not being filled, there is a mild relationship, but one leaning more to the negative side than the positive. When a weak need is not being filled, there isn't much caring either way.

When needs are not being filled by the other people or person in the relationship, there ultimately comes a parting of the ways; the manner of the parting and the stress, anger, and resentment involved pretty much depend on the strength of the unfilled need. With a strong unfulfilled need there is much anger and resentment, since the strength of the need determines the emotional force generated. With a weak unfulfilled need there is very little emotional energy and so no anger or resentment is generated beyond perhaps a shrug of the shoulders and a quietly muttered, "That's the way it goes."

To enhance any relationship is simple: find out what the other person needs and then fill that need.

To end a relationship the reverse is true. Find out what the other person needs and keep those needs unfilled.

It's as simple as that. The great principle of correspondence states, "As above so below, as below so above." When you know the key to happiness you have also learned the key to unhappiness. Without realizing it, when you know how to be a failure, you also know how to be a success. When you are successful at failing in relationships, you also know how to be successful at succeeding in relationships, once the concept is understood.

An individual who fails at a relationship is a person who neglects the needs of the partner. So it would follow that the first step to a successful relationship is to determine what needs the other person has. It is also vital to understand your own needs so that you can help the other person in the relationship to fill your needs.

Unfortunately not only do the great majority of people fail to see or to understand the other person's needs, they do not understand their own.

Children have wonderful relationships with their parents as long as their great needs are being filled. When the needs are unfulfilled, the relationship changes and problems arise. As the child grows, needs change; it is essential that the parent recognize the changes. As it is with the child to the parent, so it is with the parent to the child.

When we ask, "How can I help better this relationship?" we are asking the wrong question. To get the correct answer we have to ask the right question. A better question would be, "How can I fill this person's needs?"

Now you have a bit of detective work to do, for before any needs can be filled you must discover what those needs are. And there's the rub. For many people do not themselves know what their basic emotional needs are. And so we find ourselves with a new question to ask: "What are this person's emotional needs?"

There was a young couple at a Silva Mental Dynamics seminar who, though only recently married, were already having rough going in their relationship. After some pointed questions a seemingly insignificant incident was related. It seems that the young lady had taken archery lessons for two years in college and was rather proud of her prowess with the bow. Her husband was somewhat athletic but knew nothing of archery. She decided to teach him. Her needs at that moment were to show her love for her man, to show him that she had more talents than he had knowledge of, to demonstrate that she was even more worthy of him than he had thought, perhaps to instill a new need in him, and maybe to develop a shared taste for the sport so that they could play it together. Her self-esteem, her ego, was high; she was satisfied with herself and could afford to show this to the man who loved her.

They went to their backyard, where she had set up a target, and showed him the basics. She proceeded to send off two arrows; one landed in the inner row just outside the black bull's-eye and the other buried itself some eight inches farther out. Not great, but not bad considering the distance she'd set.

Her husband took the bow from her, smiled, nocked an arrow, and pulled back the string, releasing it with a twang. As the first arrow hit, he swiftly set, aimed, and released another. Both arrows flew straight into the bull's-eye. Calmly he took another arrow and zing, a third bull's-eye. The young lady stood in shock, her mouth agape. Her high opinion of herself was rapidly crumbling. Here was a critical moment in their relationship, but neither of them was aware of it at the time. If he had thought for a month about all the wrong things to say at that moment, he could not have picked a worse one. "Ah, there's nothing to this arrow shooting" was the young man's statement as he dispatched what turned out to be one of her major needs.

She never again fired off another arrow. Not only that, she never participated in anything that her husband might beat her at, thereby depriving herself and her husband of many joyful moments of sharing mutual needs. All because of a man not recognizing a woman's need at a particular moment.

And so we come to that fundamental question with regard to a good relationship. "How do I discover and recognize needs? Needs in myself as well as needs in others." It is sometimes easier to recognize another person's needs; our own needs are often hidden by fear, guilt, and programming. The way to recognize needs in other people is by their response to you. When you do or say something and you get a positive response, you are well on the way to need recognition. As it is in others, so it is in yourself.

What is it you respond to in a positive manner? What do you feel good about getting and about doing? What are you totally guiltless about? What can you do with complete confidence and fearlessness? What emotional scene can you manipulate without fear or guilt? Look in these areas for your needs and you will in all probability find your answers.

When using the Silva Method for need recognition and relationship enhancement, the land of Alpha will open you to a good deal more information than a simple thoughtful moment at the Beta level of consciousness. Go to your meditative, Alpha level. When you are relaxed and free of stress, then plumb your mind for the answers. An understanding and perhaps a rereading of this chapter on relationships will enhance your abilities. As you become more and more aware of both yourself and other people, your understanding will create a tolerance and knowledge of others as well as yourself. This understanding should enable you to look for and find the needs of others, and to enrich all your relationships, whether they are with family, friends, or acquaintances.

One fundamental need is for ego strength. You can strengthen the egos of other people simply by allowing them to feel good about themselves (even if you have to manufacture a situation in which they can).

As you learn more about the needs of others, be aware that they often take insidious forms. Take the need, for instance, of a mother who believes that the only way she can get love from her children is through sympathy. And so she "acquires" an assortment of illnesses to gain that sympathy, and suddenly she "needs" to be ill.

The way for the child to fulfill the mother's need in this instance is to love and cherish her, ultimately getting her to understand that the façade of ill health is unnecessary but in the meantime understanding that to her, illness is a need.

Alcohol and drugs have been called mood changers. How much easier it is to understand their insidious effects if we alter that to need changers. Under their influence, former needs are no longer necessary and things that were not necessary suddenly become vital. Some needs are enhanced, others diminished, and some eliminated while an entirely new set of needs pops up.

Then the person sobers up or comes down from the high, and another set of needs comes into being. This roller coaster of fluctuating needs makes for a difficult period in the lives of the substance abuser's loved ones, especially when they do not recognize the cause.

So long as someone is filling the temporary needs created under the influence, the relationship between substance abuser and loved one will continue. In such a relationship, you must ask yourself whether you are willing to fill the temporary needs, thereby enabling and prolonging the problem. Why not instead create a new need? You can create needs as well as fill them. Create a need for sobriety. Make a trip of mutual discovery as to what life would be like without the opiates of alcohol and drugs.

Communication is the key to discovering what a person's needs are. Communication is the key to unlocking the person from the cell of misery. Ask this question, and expect and get an answer. What would your life—what would our lives—be like, if you did not drink/take drugs?

At this point it is vital to set goals for the person and for yourself: individual goals, and goals for the two of you: goals for the next week, the next month, a year from now, ten years from now, and even twenty years from now. Goals will give direction and create new thoughts as to how to treat the now.

Let's now see how needs can be programmed through goals.

A parent wishes for a child to play the piano and sets about making the child take lessons. The child has no interest in music, however, and the lessons start out as a chore and evolve into a battle. Eventually the piano is seen as a citadel of misery. The parent may have a need for the child to play but the child has no need whatever. How to develop a relationship between the child and the piano?

The first step is to consider how to go about developing a need in the child to play. Consider what would produce that need. It might take a prolonged series of steps. You might take the child to a few piano concerts—classical, popular, and jazz—as a first step. You are not seeking to develop a direction at this point, only an appetite. Next, you might take some simple music and unlock its mystery by showing the child something about how music is written. Demonstrate how it could be seen as a different language, a language universal in its scope. Then you might have the child write a simple tune, pick it out on the piano, and actually write it on a sheet of music paper. Once it's written, you pick it out on the piano to show the child that he or she has written something understandable. Praise the child. Praise for a child is the greatest reward that you can bestow. Soon the child will develop a greater appetite for writing music, expecting the greatest reward of all, your praise.

Always reward with praise. No matter what the music looks or sounds like, it has been created and has taken the child into the realm of creativity where the seeds of genius dwell. Those seeds when properly nourished can sprout a musical prodigy before your very eyes, for when the child develops this need for your praise, he or she will hunger for more knowledge and want to do it better. The child will want instruction and the means of self-expression. Suddenly there will be a need for musical knowledge and you will find a relationship has developed between your child and music.

Of course this is an example that could be applied to many experiences in which you might want to develop a need in people. Needs may be enhanced or diminished once the process is understood. The important thing is the concept.

Knowledge without use is a waste. Knowing that needs form the basis for relationships may be an interesting concept, but if it is not utilized then the material becomes useless. The key to that use is communication: a sit-down session between two people determined to discover their mutual needs; a discussion about which needs each is willing to fill. If there are major needs that one of the parties is unwilling to fill, then substitute needs must be brought into the discussion. (I'm not willing to fill need X, but perhaps I can do Y for you.)

During a recent Silva Mental Dynamics seminar, one of the participants stood up and yelled out, "I need to smoke a cigar while I'm watching television." Pointing to the woman sitting next to him, who had a look on her face suggesting she had just bitten into an unripe lemon, he continued, "But my wife won't let me."

Needless to say, the class erupted with laughter. After they quieted down, he was asked if there were any other needs he had that she would not fill. "Sure," he said, "lots of them. I need to play cards with my friends once in a while, but she bitches so much about it that I don't do it. I like to bowl and she doesn't. When I want to go out by myself she howls like a banshee, so I don't bowl much anymore." Seeming to get a measure of bravado, he sneered down at his wife (who now looked as though she would like to crawl into herself) and said in a loud voice, "And I'm getting sick and tired of it."

Here was a relationship heading for the rocks. "Do you ever discuss these things?" he was asked.

"Sure, all the time. I say I'm going out, or I pull out a cigar and she yells."

Obviously, what he described does not constitute a

discussion. So she was asked, "Of those three things that your husband mentioned—cigar smoking, bowling, and cards—which do you like the least?"

"Well," she said quietly, "cigars make me ill. I really can't stand the smell of them in the house. I don't like him to play cards because he stays out till early in the morning and when he loses he's a grouch for two days. Bowling gets him excited and he can't sleep when he gets home, but I guess that of the three, cigars is the worst and bowling is the best. At least he gets exercise when he goes bowling."

And then she was asked, "If he gives up cigar smoking in the house, would you be willing to let him go bowling once every week?"

Her head pumped up and down rapidly. "Gladly. If he would only stop those filthy cigars in the house, he could bowl twice a week if he wanted to."

"Hold on, we're just talking about once a week right now." Then her husband was asked, "How about it, sir? You give up cigar smoking in the house, and you get to bowl once a week. Deal?"

He looked at his wife, whose eyes were wide open as she gazed back. He turned to the instructor and said, "But she puts up just as big a fuss over bowling. I don't want a battle every time I go out."

His wife was now shaking her head in the negative. "How about it?" she was asked. "The only way this need substitution will work is if you support the new need. He is giving up the need to smoke cigars in the house. You are allowing him the need to bowl. But you must be supportive. You must see the bowling from a positive viewpoint, with a positive attitude. Instead of grumbling when he plays, from this time forward, you must show him that you actually enjoy his going out to bowl. Do you understand that?"

She indicated that she did, and later they reported that their relationship had never been better. But I could have guessed that. When they walked out of the seminar hall, she had her arm around his waist, and he was gently pulling her closer to him.

Chapter 21

SOLVING FAMILY SQUABBLES

You've learned that ego is defined in the Silva Mental Dynamics classes as your opinion of yourself. When you have a healthy ego, you have a good opinion of yourself, and when you have a poor ego, you have a weak opinion of yourself. When you have a weak opinion of yourself and believe that you are valueless, then you look to outside agencies to enhance that opinion, the supposition being that if other people tell you that you're wonderful or that you're all right, then maybe you are. And so we look for strokes from other folks.

Some people need constant reinforcement and instigate it with childish questions like, "Do you really think I'm beautiful?" "Does this suit (or blouse) look good on me?" "Did I really do that well?" "Do you really think I deserve that promotion?" "Do you really think that my cooking is great?" "Isn't this car wonderful?" "Do you really like my house?"

Those who need this constant building of their egos will respond to the compliment they elicited with something like, "Oh I'm not, you're just saying that." Thus they demand a seemingly endless stream of compliments.

Then there are those who denigrate their possessions even as they know that you will contradict them. The dialogue goes something like this: "Yeah, the car is all right, but Carl Wetherby has a red one and I think maybe I should have bought a red one." Or: "The house is fine, I guess. I should have gotten one in a better neighborhood but this was the best I could do." Or: "I guess I look all right, but I wish my nose was just a trifle narrower." And if you fail to contradict them, there is always that justification, "Ah, what do they know anyway?"

The most difficult area in which to accept a neutral or negative response is within the confines of your own family circle. The closer the family member, the more faith you invest in his or her opinion of you. When you do not get the reinforcement of your opinion of yourself (enhancement of ego) from those who are closest to you, a rift comes about that grows with each such nonreinforcement. Loving and lasting relationships are generally those in which the parties feed each other's egos.

That does not mean that people have to go around telling one another how wonderful they are. The ego is one's opinion of oneself. To feed that opinion properly you need only see the other in a positive light and as a free and equal partner. This is difficult for some people to do, especially within the hierarchy that is invariably set within the family unit, with the eldest generally at the top position and the youngest at the bottom of the heap. The eldest is not prone to give up that position and the youngest has been programmed to believe that the older one is the one to look up to. This often causes a development of deep, subconscious resentments throughout life.

Let's take the case of two brothers, Albert and Drew. Drew was born when Albert was four years old and so when Drew was four, Albert was eight, a significant difference in ages. Albert sometimes cared for his little brother, sometimes played with him, and sometimes fought with him. Of course it was never much of a contest as Albert was twice Drew's age. Time passed and Drew became fourteen years old, Albert eighteen. Drew looked up to his older brother, who was doing all the things that Drew hoped to do one day. Much of what Drew learned about older boys came from his older brother. In the meantime Albert saw Drew as the kid brother, someone to teach, manage, occasionally play with, and of course always get the better of. And every time Albert taught something to his younger brother, or beat him at something, his opinion of himself (with regard to his younger brother) was enhanced. In addition he was learning new things, things that Drew knew nothing about, almost every day.

More time passes and now Drew is eighteen and beginning to feel his oats, but of course Albert is twenty-two. Albert has graduated from college and is now gainfully employed, while Drew has just entered college. Drew not only sees his older brother as the one he has always looked up to, but now sees him as a real man as well. One day he will also have a job. But Drew never had a chance to compete with Albert; it was never a contest. And Albert always looked upon

Drew as the one who was trying to catch up but of course never would because Albert would always be older and wiser.

If you were to say that the programming of this sequence started when Drew was four and Albert eight, then we find that at this point, fourteen years of rather strong sibling programming has set in.

More time passes and now Drew is thirty-two years of age, Albert thirty-six. Virtually no difference. They are both mature, educated, married men with families of their own. But what happened to all that programming between them?

It is still locked in place in the minds of both Albert and Drew.

Is it any wonder that when family members have problems, they are stronger than, and far different from, the problems between friends or acquaintances? And is it any wonder that the solutions to those problems have to deal with a great many deep-seated, strongly programmed, and often subconscious causes?

When there is a squabble between family members, look first for the solution in the area of self-esteem, ego. Look to the opinion the family members have about themselves, and how to enhance that opinion.

And so it is that when anger, resentment, or jealousy rears up within a family unit, it is much stronger than when it comes from outside the family. How sad it is when two members of a family who really love one another (and have so very much in common to share with one another all of their lives) have a squabble because of some insignificant incident that is usually based on the threatening or perceived diminishment of one or the other's needs.

Friends can be replaced. Family members cannot. When you lose a friend, you can always find another. When you lose a brother, sister, parent, child, uncle, aunt, or cousin, that loss is impossible to replace. And yet there are so many family members in this world who are apart because of a few hastily and regrettably uttered words, words that have produced an irreconcilable split in the family unit. And neither party will seek out a remedy, although often both of them love and respect one another and each would vigorously protect the other from outside forces. Although at odds with one another within the family unit, in the context of the outside world the two members will tend to protect and defend one another. Families, towns, countries, races, religions, teams of people—all have egos in that they all have opinions of themselves or their organizations that they will look to enhance and protect.

A classic example took place in a Silva Mental Dynamics class some time ago. It came about that two sisters had argued about some incident, and had not spoken to one another for five years. Let's call them Jenny and Sue; Jenny was the sister who was in the class. During the seminar Jenny mentioned her long-standing squabble with Sue. She loved her sister and wished that they could get together but neither of them had the capacity for making the first move. The advice she was given was to use our three magic words. Three words that would bring virtually any squabbling family member back to the cozy, warm, and secure bosom of the family fold.

Jenny said, "Those three words must be "I love you," and I can't say that to my sister even though I do. You're going to tell me to call my sister and tell her I love her, but there's no way I can do that. It's impossible for me to do that."

"No," she was told, "those are not our three magic words, although they will do. We realize how difficult it is to expose yourself and lay yourself on the line like that."

Jenny was asked about the root cause of the rift, which she did not recall although she thought that an argument about something or other was at the bottom of it. She was told to go to the telephone right then and there, call her sister, and before Sue could respond, say, "Sue, this is Jenny. I want you to know that I've been thinking about that fight that we had and *I was wrong.*" If she would say those words, we told her, we would guarantee her that she would gain a sister. What a cheap price to pay for a sibling. Three words: "I was wrong."

Jenny thought she could do that. But then after thinking about it, she looked up and said, "But I wasn't wrong." At which point the entire class roared with laughter. The glee seemed to clear some of the cobwebs from Jenny's mind and she smiled sheepishly. Then she walked to the nearest phone like a woman with a definite purpose. As she'd realized suddenly, admitting she was wrong when she felt she was right would make the words even more powerful. In effect she was forgiving her sister for the incident and in doing so was releasing herself from the responsibility of the anger. If her sister stayed mad after Jenny declared herself the responsible party, the one who was wrong, then that was Sue's problem, not hers.

Her opinion of herself grew as she realized that she was admitting to a fact that she felt was the opposite of what she really felt simply to develop a more loving relationship with her sister. She walked with an air of confidence toward the telephone to make her call.

Ten minutes later Jenny returned to the hall with a grin on her face, shaking her head in wonderment. She looked at the group of people and said, "You know something? This stuff really works. Now why couldn't I have thought of that?"

Jenny could have thought of that except that her ego kept getting in the way. There are a good many ways to correct a family squabble, but over the years the one that seems to work the best is saying those three words. The only response to words like those is a loving one.

But what if you do not receive a loving response? Say the response is something like, "You're doggone right you were wrong, you're always wrong," or "Well, why did you do it? Don't do that again. I knew you were wrong," or any one of a dozen similar responses. Your answer should be one of forgiveness, for the best way to cut off anger at the source before it takes hold is to simply forgive the other person for those words. And if the words seem harsh, it's because harsh thoughts built up during the period of separation.

Once you have taken the step of saying "I was wrong," know that you have separated yourself from the problem, and if you get a response other than a loving one, then it is the other family member's problem and not yours. You have taken the step. If the wound is healed by your words, fine. If it still remains a sore spot, you have done your best to resolve the problem. You can rest easy with an enhanced opinion of yourself, for you will be the better person for it.

You might want to review the previous chapter and

recall the fact that a good relationship requires the filling of some need of the other person. Ask yourself, What does this family member need? Is there any way that you yourself can fill that need? Or can you help the family member to fill that need? If you can, you will find an immediate, positive, loving response.

Chapter 22

DEALING WITH NEGATIVE PEOPLE

The essence of understanding negativity lies in the awareness of this fact: Negative thinking is a protection against disappointment. The negative thinker expects nothing good to happen and is not disappointed when nothing good happens. Most negative thinkers develop early, but occasionally the ravages of time chip away at the positive attitude of an adult, and those who are beset by constant disappointment often turn to the protective cloak of negative thinking, thereby avoiding additional pain.

The negative thinker is never disappointed; so it would seem that negative thinking has positive results. However, there is a side effect to negative thinking. When one loses the excitement of positive expectations, life becomes dull and bland, a spiceless existence. When people have nothing to look forward to, no goals and few desires, that dullness creates an apathy that brings with it the depressive state that so many in our modern society are afflicted with. And following closely behind depression is that state of mind that preys on many of the elderly, despair. Despair is that feeling that what is desired is impossible to attain. When despair comes into people's lives, they care little for anything, feeling that anything they want will automatically be impossible to get. And so they learn to want nothing and life soon becomes no more than a waiting room for the grim reaper.

If you are not bothered by this unfortunate affliction, you probably know someone who is. The easiest way to protect yourself against people like this is to avoid them (as suggested by the second rule of happiness). Would that it were that simple! For so very often the afflicted is a loved one, a close friend, a business associate, or an acquaintance. Let us see how a negative thinker is born, for an understanding of this type of person may help you decide to what degree you may wish to be involved.

Betty W. was six years old and a more exuberant, positive, excited young lady would be hard to find. The world was bright and gay and filled with wonder. Every stroll down the street led her to a thousand new discoveries. For her, grass was always green, the sky was always blue. When she awakened in the morning, she could hardly wait to jump out of bed to see what new wonders the world held in store. How could a child like this turn into a negative thinker?

One day her mother says, "Betty, we're going to the zoo this weekend," and Betty is joyful and animated as she tells her friends all about her impending visit to the zoo. Friday evening comes and her mother says to Betty, "I'm sorry, darling, I know I promised to take you to the zoo, but Daddy has to work this weekend, and we can't go." Betty is desolate. But with her youthful energy she bounces back and is her old self once again by Sunday. A few weeks go by and Betty's mother says to her joyfully, "Honey, I know we disappointed you about the zoo but this time for sure we're going for a picnic in the park on Sunday." And Betty jumps into the air with a great "Hooray!" and runs to tell her friends. Saturday comes and Betty's mother says, "I'm terribly sorry, Betty, but I forgot we're going to Grandma's house and can't go on the picnic."

Now Betty loves her grandmother dearly, but if she were to weigh going to grandmother's against a picnic in the park, Grandma would lose every time. And once again Betty is disappointed.

It won't happen the second time, the fifth time, perhaps not even the twentieth time, but at some future time Betty will respond to her mother's invitation something like this: Mother says, "Betty, we're going to the amusement park this weekend," and Betty says in reply, "Aw, it'll probably rain, Mother, or Daddy will have to work, or maybe I'll get sick." And another negative thinker has been born.

Betty has learned that disappointment hurts. She does not want to be hurt anymore and so has figured out for herself that if she does not expect good things to happen, she will not be disappointed when they don't, and therefore will not be hurt.

Understanding that negative people are people who have had a great many disappointments in their life brings you to a better awareness of why they think as they do. Negative thinking has taken a great deal of programming and reinforcement through the years to produce. It is unlikely that you are going to turn negative thinkers around with a few words. You can, however, put them on the road back to the positive methods of Silva by reversing the process. Negative thinkers are born through disappointment. The way to turn negative thinkers around is to make sure that you personally never disappoint them.

Many of our Silva graduates who have loved ones in rest homes or other institutions for the aged have discovered that for the most part an aura of negativity hangs over the place like a low cloud of smog, infecting everyone inside. Those who make the attempt to turn someone around face a formidable task—formidable, but nevertheless possible. The feedback that we've gotten from graduates of our program tells us it can be done by reversing the method it took to turn six-year-old Betty into a negative thinker.

Call your institutionalized loved one on the telephone or write and set an exact time that you will be there to visit. Be there at that time. When leaving, make up a strange time for your return visit. Say something like, "Dear, I'm visiting a friend in the neighborhood next Tuesday and I have to leave there at twelve. I'll be here to see you on Tuesday at twelve-seventeen." Make sure that you both have the same time, and make doubly sure that you're there at precisely 12:17. It will take a while, but one day your loved one will begin to come back to life. "You know," you might hear, "the food tastes a little better." Suddenly, appetites begin to return, not necessarily just for food but for experience, for change, for a grain of excitement.

It's unlikely that negative thinkers will turn into Pollyannas, but your goal should be to carry them as far from despair as possible.

What of those people you feel are impossible to change? For that is what you have just attempted to do, change your loved one. Then there are those people who are not loved ones but who you do not wish to avoid, for whatever reason (for avoidance is easy). If you simply avoid a negative person, then of course you've rid yourself of the problem. Determine the relationship between yourself and the negative person. It may be that you have a subconscious need to torment yourself due to some recent or long-forgotten guilt. (See Chapter 8, "Guilt and Self-Forgiveness.")

All people have problems that you are not aware of, problems that affect their viewpoint, attitudes, and expectations. You will be better equipped to help those people as well as yourself by using the visual images of the positive thinker and our dynamic Silva methods.

PART SIX

Work and Business

Chapter 23

SETTING AND ACHIEVING GOALS

When you want to grow a turnip yourself instead of purchasing the vegetable at your local market, the first thing you must do is to get yourself some turnip seeds. You must then find a plot of soil, prepare the ground, dig a hole, put in the seeds, cover them up, water them, and fertilize them. Then nature takes over and the seeds sprout, grow, and eventually produce your turnips.

The plot of ground that you plant the seeds in should be in a location that gets lots of sunlight, for if you plant the seeds in a cellar you will find the seedlings stunted and warped, if indeed they grow at all. And if you do not see to it that they get water, they will die. If you put them into uncultivated hard ground, they will not be able to break through. Neglect to fertilize them and they will grow poorly.

It takes a bit of thought and preparation before you can turn a turnip seed into a fully mature turnip, and

217

so it is with programming goals, for programming is the same as seeding the ground for turnips.

As it is with seeding, so it is with programming; both are desires for a specific cause to manifest into a specific effect. How does the seeding process apply to people?

Mark H. was sixteen years old when he decided that he wanted to play the piano. He asked for and got a piano from his parents after promising to take lessons and practice diligently. (The decision to play was the decision to acquire the seeds. The goal was set.) The piano arrived. (And so he had the ground that he wanted to plant the seeds in. But it was still dry, hard, shady ground.) His parents lined up a piano instructor for Mark, and so he now had his seeds.

The day he began his lessons was the day the ground was prepared and the seeds planted. (He now had to nurture them, to water them, and to fertilize and weed the seedlings as they took root and grew.) He diligently practiced every day, for unless he went forward daily, he felt that he would slip back a bit. (A few days without water would not kill the seedling turnips, but it might stunt them.) As he practiced he learned new things and developed new ideas about music. Each new plateau showed him how much there was still to learn, and the more he learned, the more he began to appreciate how infinite knowledge truly is. But as his capacity grew so did his appetite; and the seeds—prepared, planted, and nurtured—grew to magnificent fruition. At age twenty-two, Mark H. gave his first professional concert and was rewarded with accolades and applause. He had seeded his future correctly.

Benson G., however, was a different story. Benson was also sixteen when he decided that it might be nice to play the piano. Every time he saw or heard anyone playing the piano, he imagined that he was playing. He daydreamed about it and badgered his mother with requests to buy a piano. Finally she purchased a spinet. It sat in a corner of the living room, and every now and again Benson sat down and banged out something like a tune.

One day his mother arranged for an instructor to teach her son the basics of piano, but Benson always had something else that he would rather do than go to a lesson. He practiced every now and again, but instead of concentrating on the now, on what he was doing, he fantasized about being a great pianist. (He had acquired the seeds, but had thrown them on top of the ground with no preparation, no nurturing and no water, and in shady ground. The turnips never had a chance.) All his life he had this desire to play the piano. But he cared for the seeds improperly.

The seeding of cause for desired effect is quite simple and can be summed up with five rules.

1. Decide what you want to plant and acquire the seeds. (If you purchase carrot seeds you will be disappointed if you expect turnips to sprout.)

2. Prepare the ground. (Professionals take more time in preparation than they do in the actual work. The amateur looks to cut corners and skip preparation. You must break up the soil, plow the ground, hoe it, scatter nutrition, and water it if you expect a bountiful crop.)

3. Plant the seed. (Begin. The seeds will not sprout in their envelope or in your pocket. There's no need to concern yourself with whether or not they will germinate and grow, for if you do not plant them, they will surely not grow.)

4. Tend it. (You must weed, thin, water, and fertilize if you expect a good strong crop.)

5. Harvest. (The ideal time to harvest the crop is at its peak. This is the time when you must decide whether to pick the fruit of your toil and enjoy it.)

When you do this seeding exercise, go to level and decide what goal you'd like to program for. The five rules to a good crop constitute the procedure you'll follow to attain your goal.

Let's say you've decided to program for painting your house. First you will see yourself acquiring seeds, in this case the paint, roller, and brushes. You will then visualize yourself preparing the ground, or preparing for the activity that you are programming for. Visualize yourself covering the furniture, scraping where necessary, masking off windows, removing doors, and moving books, pictures, and furniture. Next, visualize yourself planting the seeds: see yourself beginning. The furniture is rearranged, the masking tape is up, and the plastic tarp has been laid; you start painting.

Finally, mentally see yourself picking the fruits of whatever you have planted. Picture the paint job finished, the furniture put back, the house looking fresh and well kept. Whatever goal you are programming yourself to attain, now picture yourself having made it part of you; you're satisfied with your involvement and in total control to continue or to change whenever you choose.

Seeding is an excellent method of motivating yourself to be goal-oriented and to complete jobs you've started.

Chapter 24

COMMUNICATION

The principle of gender states that all things have masculine and feminine aspects and that the masculine is the outgoing, the instigative force, while the feminine is the incoming, the receptive, the creative force. These forces are basic, intrinsic to everything from the smallest molecule to the universe itself. These forces, which some call "yang" and "yin," carry no values; neither one is good or bad, but both are necessary parts of all existence. Nor do the masculine and feminine forces have anything to do with the male or female sex, although man and woman are manifestations of the law of gender on the physical plane.

Communication is easier to understand when applying this principle, for when you speak with someone, you are, to some degree, in the masculine or outgoing mode, and when you're listening you are in the receptive, the inflowing, the feminine mode. To understand, indeed even to hear what is being said by the other person, you must be in the receptive/ feminine mode. To have others understand what you are saying you must be in the outgoing/masculine mode. Just as a magnet will attract another magnet only when the outgoing/masculine pole is put together with the receptive/feminine pole, so it is with communication. If you were to speak from the receptive mode to a listener also in the receptive mode, you would get a repelling force. When you put the outgoing with the outgoing, you again have a repelling force. To get adherence (communication), you must have positive with negative, the receptive with the outgoing.

When two people are attempting to communicate and both are in the outgoing mode, when each has something to say and is eager to say it, there is no communication and therefore no understanding. When two people are in the receptive mode and they each wish to hear what the other one has to say, then again, there is no communication. For there to be any effective movement of information between two people, the speaker to some degree must be in the outgoing mode, and the listener in the receptive/ inflowing.

You will find this principle at work in all forms of endeavor—in writing, painting, and all of the other arts; you'll find the principle at work in sports, in business, and in all the professions. To locate this force you have only to be aware of its existence.

Popular leaders have developed a strong outgoing force when speaking. Immensely masculine, sending out a heroic force, they overcome the masculine energy fields of the crowd and switch them to the receptive. (Remember, this has nothing to do with sex. A woman can project the masculine, or outgoing, force just as easily as a man.) New lines of communication open and great masses of people are swayed by the charisma of the speaker. Charisma is an extremely strong outgoing force.

As in all things, the degree of the force varies. Two speakers, both essentially the same but one of them in better command of the audience and so displaying a higher degree of the outgoing power, will have different effects on the listeners. By better command, we mean a strong sense of self-confidence, which in turn usually comes from knowledge of the material, practice, and previous exposure to a similar circumstance with a positive result. There are also those who have a strong sense of self-confidence for other reasons and whose strong ego manifests as charisma.

Notice how the people you find to be charismatic and influential seem to be in command. There are salespeople, attorneys, stockbrokers, accountants, doctors, politicians, and coworkers who cause you to do something without question, or perhaps to question it but do it anyway. If they have any degree of control over you, you can bet that they have the outgoing force about them (at least with respect to you).

Edward S., a recent student of the Silva Mental Dynamics seminar, heard this information and said that he suddenly understood one of his employees who had him totally confused. The sales manager for a major encyclopedia firm, Edward supervised an incredibly successful salesman by the name of Big John Jones. Big John was just that: at six feet seven inches and 325 pounds, he was a very impressive sight to behold. It seemed that nearly every time he made a call, Big John sold a set of encyclopedias.

Big John was so successful that Edward decided to make him head of the outside sales department and train other salespeople. The first day a man went out with Big John he reported to Edward that Big John was a mediocre salesman and that he didn't want to go out with him again. The man was asked if Big John sold a set of books. "Yes," he was told, "he sold a set. But I don't know how he did it. He's one of the worst salesmen I've ever seen."

Needless to say, Edward did not lend too much credence to that report. The next day he sent another man out with Big John. The second man gave the same appraisal of Big John's selling ability. Edward asked if he sold any books. "Yes, he sold a set. But I don't know how; he gave a lousy presentation."

Mystified now, Edward decided to accompany Big John that evening while he went out on a call, and sure enough he heard his prize salesman deliver a rambling presentation, an inept close, and a sale of a mid-priced bound set of encyclopedias.

But Big John was such an overwhelming masculine presence, Edward came to realize, that he was causing his clients to switch to the receptive mode and surrender at the sight of him. When Big John rang the doorbell, the client would come to the door, take one look at that mass of towering masculine strength on the doorstep, switch to the inflowing feminine mode, and surrender. With Big John not only physically outgoing but also confident of success, he had only to ask for a signature to make the sale; his presentation was incidental to his close. Edward said that he actually got a call from a woman one day who said, "Your man was at my house last night and I bought something. Tell me, what did I buy?"

Have you ever purchased something you did not really want just to get away from a salesperson? If you did, you can bet that you were in the feminine/receptive mode and the salesperson was in the masculine/outgoing.

There is a way to control this force.

The next time you're dealing with a salesperson (or for that matter, with any domineering person), recognize the fact that successful salespeople are always in the masculine mode. For you to be in a buying spirit, you must be in a feminine mode. You can switch yourself to either mode. If you wish to listen to the sales presentation, imagine that you are in the receptive mode, with things coming to you. Picture the incoming ocean tide, or someone throwing a ball to you, or a car driving along a street toward you, anything that is incoming relative to yourself. See yourself purchasing the product or service and being happy with it. You can see how useful this would be to students listening to an instructor and wanting to retain the information better. A student who is sitting in a classroom and thinking about other things is usually in the outgoing mode, and is getting little from the teacher's lessons. To switch to the feminine/receptive so as to have a better understanding and superior retention of the material, the student should consider incoming things. It is always best to put the first three fingers of either hand together to trigger the mind into paying attention to the program.

If you would like to have more control over the outgoing mode and to stop the receptivity, switch to the masculine. First, visualize a protective shield between yourself and the person you're dealing with. This shield absorbs all the incoming masculine energy before it can envelop you. Next, visualize yourself in the outgoing mode. Picture yourself speaking forcefully. Picture things going away from you; imagine a train, a rocket, a boat, or any other vehicle moving away from you. See yourself in action—perhaps turning your back on the person, or walking away, or closing the door on the man or woman in front of you. Most physical actions put you in the outgoing mode.

If it is a salesperson whose outgoing mode you'd like to control, remember that you are in charge; you need make no excuses for declining to purchase anything. Say, "No, I've decided that now is not the time," or simply, "No, I do not want it."

If the salesperson asks you any question, such as why not, and you answer the question, you will place yourself back in the feminine mode. You do not have to justify your reasons. You do not have to have any reasons. Your answer to the question should simply be, "I just don't want it, no reasons." It's as simple as that.

We recognize that sometimes it is difficult to get away from the clutches of a forceful salesperson or an overly aggressive family member, friend, or colleague who is in the masculine mode, especially when you find it difficult to get out of the feminine mode. Here is an easy technique for you to use.

You have just visualized a force leaving you, an arrow being shot from a bow, a rocket going away from you, a car racing away, or anything outgoing. And then you have said to the salesperson, "I've changed my mind, I don't want it."

At this point you will be asked what made you change your mind, or why don't you want it, or any question to keep you engaged. It doesn't matter what the salesperson asks; answer any question by responding, "Why do I have to answer that question?"

And you will see someone practically melt before your eyes. To understand your question, the salesperson will have to switch to the feminine/receptive mode. When that happens, any power he or she had over you has vanished. Then you may smile nicely and leave.

All forceful people are outgoing. Who's the outgoing/masculine force in your life? Your mother-in-law, spouse, boss, parent, child? Most authority figures are seen as masculine forces, and we tend to switch to the receptive when in their presence. Use your knowledge of the forces of gender to control the masculine and feminine modes within yourself and to understand and enhance your communication with others.

Chapter 25

A MINI-COURSE IN BUSINESS SUCCESS

In this chapter we'll cover ten areas crucial to success in business: motivation, advancing company goals, developing clear thought, taking effective action, sales, overcoming the fear of rejection, brainstorming for new ideas to promote company success, relaxation and stress management, the positive salesperson, and building a dynamic, ambitious, goal-oriented company team.

You might think that this is an ambitious project to handle in one chapter. But as you'll see, most of these ten points relate to Silva Mental Dynamics concepts already covered in previous chapters. When you put all ten points together, you'll find that whatever business you are in, including the business of working for someone else, they will help you in your future endeavors.

1. Motivation. If you view problems as challenges and goals rather than overwhelming burdens, you'll find yourself taking action more readily. Procrastination, the opposite of motivation, stems from a lack of desire. To motivate yourself, you must enhance your desire. (See Chapter 18, "Motivation and Procrastination.") There is no such thing as failure and therefore no reason for you to put off doing whatever you wish to motivate yourself to do. (See Chapter 26, "Personal Business Success.")

2. *Advancing company goals.* Before you can advance a goal, you have to determine what that goal is. Write down all of the goals for your company with the desired completion dates. Go to level and visualize the positive end result of the goal accomplished. Bring in mental images of how the success of the goal stimulates new ideas for company growth. Apply the programming techniques to the effort to attain them as described in Chapter 11 on past programming, Chapter 26 on personal business success, and Chapter 20 on relationships, in that order.

3. *Developing clear thought.* Clear thought is developed by concentrating on a particular thought to the exclusion of all others. All of our geniuses had the ability to concentrate totally. Among the many stories about Albert Einstein is one that has him walking down a path in Princeton when he was stopped by a colleague. After a brief conversation Einstein asked the fellow, "Tell me, when you stopped me, was I heading away from my home or toward it?" His colleague replied, "Why, away from it." Stroking his chin thoughtfully, Einstein said, "Ah, then I've already had lunch." Now that is concentration of thought.

How do we gain such concentration? Through first-stage meditation, as described in Chapter 1. Once you are at your meditative level, then and only then should you develop the idea that you are utilizing the meditation for. To further clarify the thought, bring in the enhanced visualization that we call Golden Images as described in Chapter 5.

4. Taking effective action. Business success depends on carrying out actions designed to stimulate the business. You cannot take effective action unless you take some action. Nothing on earth has been accomplished that has not had a beginning. The only true failure is not to begin. For beginning that action and then ensuring its effectiveness, we recommend reading Chapter 18, "Motivation and Procrastination"; Chapter 23, "Setting and Achieving Goals"; and Chapter 26, "Personal Business Success."

5. Sales. Now we come to a very concise sales course. We will assume you know your product and can give a presentation about it. Let us say that the presentation takes 90 percent of your time. That allots 10 percent to sales, and by sales we mean closing the sale. For unless you can close the sale, you are a conversationalist, not a salesperson.

When you complete the presentation, you *must* qualify the customers—that is, induce them to affirm their desire for your product. To do that, there must be a qualifying question. This is not the same as the prequalification, when you discover whether or not they like and can afford your product. There is no point in trying to sell a $60,000 Porsche to someone who has no money saved and earns $300 a week. After the prequalification and presentation comes the time for the qualification.

The qualifying question is this: "Mr. Prospect,

would you appreciate having this product [this service, this whatever] if time and money were not a consideration?"

When customers answer yes, they have taken mental possession of the product. All you have to do at this point is to wrap up the sale by showing them how to purchase it.

Once you ask the qualifying question and get a positive response, you go into your close. You do not go back to the presentation or you will lose the sale.

If they say no to your qualifying question, you might just as well wrap it up, for you haven't done your job in the presentation or in prequalifying them. If they don't want to buy, do not waste any more time with them. You just asked if they want the product or service free, with no time constraints. If they say no to that, then nothing you're going to say will sell them.

The qualification is vital to all sales presentations, because once customers have taken mental possession of a product, then in their own minds they already own it. When you asked that question, a visualization of them owning the item flashed in their minds; mentally they already own it. When you get a yes to your qualifying question, assume that you have the sale and write up the order.

If there are any objections at this point, it is usually because the customers do not know how to go about buying the product. Your job is to make it as easy as possible. We're going to refer to two methods of sale. One is called "purchasing on a minor issue." The other is "not giving them the option to say no."

Let me explain purchasing on a minor issue. Whatever you are selling, have something else available at an extremely low price by comparison and make sure that it goes along with the item for sale. If you're a car salesman selling a $12,000 car, for example, see to it that you have a selection of hood ornaments or special hubcaps for the customers to choose from. The hood ornaments, let's say, cost $10. After they have said yes to your qualifying question but before you write up the sale for the automobile, have them pick their choice of ornament. Offer them a variety to choose from—silver, gold, large, small. When they have made their selection of the $10 ornament, they have also bought themselves a $12,000 car.

If you're selling a house, see to it that something about the house or something in the house can be purchased in addition to the house for a lower price—$100, $500, $1,000. Sell that. When they've purchased the minor issue offer, they've also bought the house.

Regarding the second method, how do you remove their option to say no? For one thing, do not ask your customer, "Would you like to buy this?" If you do, you are opening yourself to the easiest response, "No." If you're selling something, whether it's yourself to a child, a product to a customer, or a service to a client, always speak in a way that makes it difficult to say no. Do not give the customers the option of saying no. Say, for instance, you're selling a couch. After you've prequalified your customer and asked the qualifying question, see to it that you show two or three colors. Then, instead of saying, "Do you want to purchase this couch?" you put it in this manner: "Would you like the red couch or the green couch?

Would you like the brown pillows or the white pillows? Do you wish it delivered on Tuesday or on Saturday? Are you going to pay by check or by credit card?" Always give them a choice where the answer cannot be a no.

A woman who worked in an ice cream shop did very well selling eggs in milkshakes. Her business boomed because there was a great deal of profit in selling the eggs. No one else ever sold an egg in a milkshake, but she invariably did. She asked a very simple question to the purchaser of every milkshake. When someone sat down and said, "I'll have a chocolate milkshake," she'd reply with enthusiasm, "Yes, sir, would you like one egg or two in it?" She sold a lot of eggs in milkshakes.

6. *Overcoming the fear of rejection.* If anything is the bane of the sales profession, it is the fear of rejection. To overcome this fear, read once again the story of Shawn and changing your viewpoint in Chapter 2. Read about self-esteem in Chapter 10; and then read the story of Friend and Hostile in Chapter 13, which deals with changing the past self's image. With your understanding of the concepts, you'll soon find that rejection is only a word for you in a dictionary.

7. *Brainstorming for new ideas to promote company success.* Brainstorming requires more than one person. Get as many people involved as you can, up to a dozen. Have everyone sit around a table and have them come up with any idea that they can think of to advance the company goals. Nothing is to be laughed at. Fantasy is fine. One thing leads to another, and inside of half an hour you find suddenly the brain-

storming pays off with an idea that will benefit the company. It is important when brainstorming to have everyone understand that anything at all that might enhance sales can be proposed; no matter how ridiculous it seems, every idea will be thought about and discussed. You will find this a great trigger device for ideas and creative thought.

8. Relaxation and stress management. Make it your company policy for all employees to take a fifteen-minute relaxation break every day. Have them go to level at some convenient time. You will find an immediate increase in productivity and creative ideas. If you work for someone else, make it your own personal policy to go to level at least once each day during work hours. (See Chapter 1, "First-Stage Meditation," and Chapter 6, "Stress.")

9. The positive salesperson. Teach all sales personnel the value of positive thinking. Get them to compete with themselves. Set positive goals for them to increase the percentage of their successful sales or to see more customers. (See Chapter 10, "Self-Esteem.")

10. Building a dynamic, ambitious, goal-oriented company team. Have your entire team read this book and you will create a dynamo of enthusiastic, ambitious salespeople. After they have read and discussed the Silva Mental Dynamics material, gather them all together for a creative brainstorming session.

By following all ten points, you will find your business acumen increasing and your limitations disappearing. If you have a viable idea or business, these pointers must help you to be successful. It is always better if you go over any tip, idea, or point of interest at the meditative Alpha level of mind before making any decisions. After reading each of the ten points and the chapters, if any, each point refers you to, go to level, consider your thoughts about that particular point, and then act on your decision.

Chapter 26

PERSONAL BUSINESS SUCCESS

Business is defined as the occupation, profession, or trade in which you are engaged. For purposes of this discussion, let us look at your occupation as your business. With what are you occupied? What is it that consumes your time—self-employment, a partnership, a corporation? Your business could be commerce, manufacturing, wholesaling, retailing, or a service. Teaching could be regarded as business as a teacher is occupied in education. Selling and buying is business. Likewise, business could be a thing that you do just for the love of it or anything that keeps you occupied. Housekeeping could be your business if you are a homemaker; typing and filing if you are a secretary; hairdressing if you are a beautician; medical care of people if you're a nurse. Writing could be business to an author, painting or sculpting to an artist.

Whatever your business is, it should be recognized

for the integral part it plays in your life. You should do your best to make this activity stress free. Be happy, be joyful, enjoy your business. An important way to live a happier, more joyful, and longer life is to avoid stress. The best manner in which to avoid stress is to work in a job or business that you truly enjoy. If you do not like your business, then you should choose either to change your business or to adjust your viewpoint of that business.

How can you improve your business so that you enjoy it more, so that you can work with a greater feeling of joy and gain? First, develop a more positive attitude toward your business by developing new and affirmative goals which, when acted upon, will create a fresh enjoyment and exciting enthusiasm for you.

Begin thinking of what those goals would be. Many people avoid starting new ventures because they are afraid of failing, not realizing that the only real failure is in not starting in the first place. For not to begin is never to finish and, hence, not to succeed. There can be no success if there is no beginning, as there is no birth without conception, no eagle without an egg, no plant without a seed. If you do not start, you have already failed.

There can be no failure once you have begun when you understand that lessons can be learned from every experience. Thomas Edison, when working on experiments that led to the electric light bulb, had more than a thousand "failures," or at least that was what his contemporaries said. When asked by a colleague why he continued his pursuit of the elusive filament after so many failures, he replied, "Why, we have not had any failures. We now know of a thousand things that don't work." Successful people see each "failure" as a learning experience.

To improve your viewpoint of your business, strive to become more creative in the things that you do. Creativity results from self-generated impulses under your control. The outer conscious self is capable of stimulating the inner self into obeying its orders. By simply saying to yourself or, more to the point, to your inner self, "Today I will be more creative"—or if you prefer to identify your inner self, "Today *we* will be more creative!"—wheels will start rolling, producing the creativity you desire. Creativity can be enhanced and stimulated by placing the first three fingers of either hand together and thinking the words, "I am going to be more creative; I am more creative." By being more creative in your occupation, you will find your awareness increasingly heightened; you will be like a butterfly emerging from a cocoon as you establish more expansive and ambitious goals for yourself.

What is the height of your desire with respect to your present occupation or business? Consider what you would want out of your business if you could gain the ultimate. Now imagine ten times that ultimate. Remove all feelings of doubt and limitation. What would be the very highest conceivable form of the occupation with which you are involved? If you are a sculptor, it might be that a piece you have completed has been chosen to represent the entire world; it might be that you, as a sculptor, have been chosen to represent the entire galaxy or the whole universe and that beings beyond our dimension are interested in your work. Allow your imagination to run free. If you are a business person, think of the ultimate, removing all restraints from your imagination. Take it beyond the local, regional, national, the international scene. What is holding you back? Where do your limitations lie?

Ask yourself this question: "If I had no limitations whatever with respect to my business, if I had unlimited funds, if I had worldwide contacts, both social and business, where would my occupation lead, in what direction would it grow, into what would it evolve?" Think about your ultimate goal. Think about a goal that would be the ultimate if all these forces were at work. Now that you have established a top goal, you can structure your desired goals. How far are you now from your ultimate goal?

Build yourself a symbolic ideal. Draw a pyramid on a piece of paper. The base of the structure represents where you are at the present time; the peak of the pyramid is your ultimate, idealistic goal. This ideal, however, is never attained. It is something to strive for, not to reach, for the closer you get to the ideal, the more your concept of the ideal changes. Knowing that the ultimate goal is something you will never reach enables you to set other goals that *are* reachable. Climb your pyramid a stone at a time, setting realistic goals; each plateau you reach enables you to visualize and gain the next.

Let us suggest that the figure of one thousand represents your ideal—one thousand words, services, thoughts, people, or whatever. This represents your unreachable star. At present, let us say that you are at the figure three. Your immediate goal is to get into the area of ten, and then the twenties, thirties, and forties until you reach the number one hundred. When you reach one hundred, you strive for one hundred twenty-five, one hundred fifty; your next goal is one hundred seventy-five, then two hundred, two hundred fifty, three hundred, and so on. Whereas one thousand seemed inaccessible when you began at three, it has now become very accessible at three hundred.

And when it happens that you do reach seven or eight hundred, you will find that the one-thousand goal is no longer your ideal; it will have changed as you have changed. As you have grown and now find one thousand reachable, your ideal becomes five or ten thousand. Whatever these numbers represent to you, the way becomes easier when you seek to do just a bit better than you have done before. A building is built a brick at a time; a book is written a sentence at a time. It is difficult for a nonwriter to conceive of a finished book, but not the finished sentence; if the book represents the ideal, the sentence is the beginning. If the building is the ideal, the first brick is the beginning. Without a beginning, there can be no successful ending; there can be no resolution whatever.

Consider the reasons that you have not begun if, in fact, you have not. Could it be that the dream is more desirable than the attainment of the goal? After all, the dream in itself requires no work, no beginning, and no struggles toward plateaus; the dream generally begins with the ideal. With the dream there can be no failure; of course neither can there be success. By not starting, the dream remains intact. Taking the first step turns the dream into reality. Does the thought of the dream being destroyed overcome your desire to begin? Think about what it is that keeps you from taking that first step.

Reflect on motivation or the incentive to act. Utilize the principle of polarity by thinking of the opposite of motivation, the absence of incentive, or weak desire or procrastination. If procrastination is your problem, it remains for you to build desire by stretching forth. One builds desire by identifying and understanding one's values and goals, by developing an ideal and reaching for it.

One of the problems that many business people have, in whatever occupation or profession, is that of decision making. Many times, the right decision is not that far from the wrong one and the only really wrong decision is not making a decision at all. If you have a decision to make and the ultimate outcome of that decision will not influence your ideal, what is the real significance of that decision? Get into the habit of instant decision making and you will find it a powerful force in your race to the top.

Once there was a captain of industry who had the reputation of instant decision making. When one of his executives would come to him with a problem, he would think momentarily, one hand in his jacket pocket and the other rubbing his chin, as he stared at the ceiling. After a moment more, he would look into the eyes of the one asking for advice and give a negative or positive answer with such authority that the man would leave shaking his head in wonderment at the supreme confidence of his boss.

Time and again, his ability to make immediate decisions helped the company to achieve new heights in that industry. Stories were told about his uncanny ability to make the right decision instantly. His reputation grew until the aura around him was almost mystic. One day the head of his marketing department came to him and laid out a new campaign. The captain of industry looked at the projections, asked a few questions, thought for a few moments, and said, "Yes, let's go ahead with it." Another time he was asked about a problem with the company cafeteria. Suggestions were made about moving it to another area. He asked a few questions and said, "Leave it where it is."

Instant and emphatic decisions, no hemming and hawing, no procrastinating, never a request to sleep on it, and always a definite answer in moments—his reputation grew to the point where he was looked upon as a seer. Other captains of industry envied his ability and, on the day of his retirement, called to ask his secret. He politely requested that his response be kept within the confines of the company. The new chief executive officer, as he took over the position, asked the retiring CEO for the secret. When they were alone in the office, the retiring chief executive officer smiled at the new CEO and said, "Beans."

The new officer looked quizzically at his friend, thinking he had not heard correctly. "One more time?" he said.

"Beans" was the reply.

"Beans?" the new officer asked. "I don't understand."

The retiring executive pulled a handful of beans out of his pocket and let them fall from one hand to the other and then put them back in his pocket. "I discovered a long time ago that when I put off a decision, the problem invariably got worse. So I devised a method of making an instant decision. I got a pocketful of beans and whenever I was asked for an answer that could be answered in the negative or in the positive, I would reach in and grab a few. I counted them out with my hand in my pocket, and if the number was odd, I would say "no"; if the number was even, my answer would be "yes."

"You see," he continued, "it really didn't make any difference what I said; the thing that did make a difference was not putting the decision off. Oh, sure, I was wrong sometimes, but, right or wrong, the decision was made and I could put my energies into something of real importance."

"Beans," the new executive said, shaking his head.

The retiring captain of industry reached over to the new captain of industry, who stood with hand stretched out, and spilled a handful of beans into the new chief executive's hand with a smile, saying, "Here's your ticket to a great reputation, Bob. Use them wisely."

And with a shake of his head, he left the office for his well-deserved retirement.

PART SEVEN

Change

Chapter 27

THE CHALLENGE OF CHANGE

You're going through a transitional time in your life and you are not sure about what to do. It's a major turning point. Whatever you decide will affect the rest of your life, as well as the lives of other people, some of whom you know and some of whom you do not yet know. You must determine whether this change will be a benefit for you and your loved ones. There will be an effect on your future even if you do nothing.

If you do nothing, things will continue as they are. Think about that. Do you want things to continue as they are? Look at your current situation in two ways, from a positive viewpoint and then from a negative viewpoint. First, imagine the present continuing as it is now, but sense yourself accepting conditions; imagine yourself seeing the positive nature of all the things that are disturbing at the present time. Imagine the way things will be if you allow them to continue with no changes. What are the positive aspects of that eventuality?

Next, view the negative side of all the things that disturb you at present. Imagine your circumstances if you allow them to continue the way they are now. What will be the outcome of this continuation?

Think back to a period in the past when the problems you seek to resolve first developed. Was your viewpoint different then? Do the things that disturbed you then leave you unconcerned today? Have you yourself changed? Change is growth. If you yourself have changed, consider the fact that you may have matured and outgrown your present situation.

Project yourself into the future and imagine what it would be like with an entirely different situation. Would you be happy with this new situation? Would your loved ones be happy with this new situation?

Change involves establishing new patterns and breaking old ones. An established pattern, or habit, is comforting because it is familiar (even when there are unwelcome results). It's easy to attach yourself to comfort. In addition, familiarity carries a measure of security; you feel secure because you know the territory.

Repetition of any activity breeds familiarity. When you do a job you're familiar with, it becomes routine. Routine is comforting because you know what's ahead.

Just as a child (who undergoes constant change and growing awareness) requires a familiar object about at all times, so does the adult. The only difference is in the type of object. It takes a great deal of maturing before the child is willing to let go of the familiar object. It doesn't matter in the least that the object may be unwashed, smelly, scratchy, or full of lumps.

What does matter is that it is familiar, and that is comforting. Any attempt to remove the familiar before the child is willing to let go leads to chaos. But if you allow the child to develop to a point where the letting go becomes a plateau of growth, you will see a beneficial crossroads in the life of that youngster.

We all have security blankets that we hang on to with fists of iron. Fearful of letting go of the familiar, we accept the continuing routine of things that someone on the outside might see as unacceptable. The outsider, not understanding that the seemingly negative experience represents security, will come up with false conclusions every time. Lacking information, the outsider cannot possibly understand what is going on. Even the person with the problem may not realize that the situation is necessary, that it represents the security of the familiar.

Most of us attribute to outside agencies the forces that direct us to failure or success. When we feel that we have no control over these forces, then change becomes a throw of the dice. Not wanting to gamble on change and perhaps lose the security of the familiar, we remain in the comforting place known as the status quo (the existing state of affairs).

Actually, there is no sense in worrying about or concentrating on past mistakes. For given the same information and the same you of that time, you would find that if you could relive the event you would do the same thing all over again. The reason you are seeing it as an error is that you have grown and are no longer the same person that you were then.

Look at things not as mistakes, but as guideposts showing you the way to a better place. See all things as experience. Your mistakes are only things that did not work. The only way for you to know what works is to do. If something does not work, it's up to you not to use it again. Keep at it until you discover what does work. Persistence is the key.

To gain the strength necessary to view change as growth, as fruitful and challenging, you must view change as a positive experience (providing, of course, that the change is desired). By relaxing and bringing into your consciousness the dynamic visualization of the positive aspects of that change, you begin the process.

Do something right now. Begin by enjoying something. Begin now. Let the next moment just happen. Enjoy it for itself. Whatever you are doing, enjoy the doing.

Now relax. When you are relaxed, all your energies are flowing properly and in accord with one another. You are in balance.

Anxiety vanishes when you are relaxed. Anxiety is a form of fear, apprehension about some future event. You cannot be fearful of a future event if you expect that event to be positive. The fear of change stems from expecting something bad to happen.

When you fear the future, things of the past appear more desirable. Older people, seeing only decay in the future, fear it, feeling that any change will be negative; they dream of the past when they felt secure. The young are most resilient to change for the opposite reasons.

Change is growth. Without change there can be no strengthening of concepts, no greater awareness, no evolution. Change is a necessary part of the human experience. To avoid change is to avoid life.

By viewing change as resulting in the successful attainment of a goal, change and the future become things of great joy, and the appetite for life is strengthened and reestablished. Desired change becomes a natural thing. Change becomes something to look forward to, a positive expectation. Change becomes a belief that something beneficial is going to happen.

To instill the strength necessary to view change as growth, as fruitful and challenging, it remains only to use the Silva techniques. We view change as a positive experience, providing the change is desired. Go to level, your meditative Alpha state of mind, and visualize the change as a positive event. Use the Golden Image technique as outlined in Chapter 5 to enhance the positive image. See the end result you desire as though you were the author of a play about your life. View the positive aspects white-framed and expect good things to take place. You'll be making the unfamiliar familiar.

Change then becomes a natural thing. Change then becomes something to look forward to; a positive expectation, faith. Change then becomes a belief that something good is about to happen.

Believe it to be and it will be.

How To Balance Your Mind With

The Silva Mind Control Method

José Silva and Philip Miele

The Silva Mind Control Method developed by José Silva has met with world-wide acclaim and today boasts millions of users around the world. Its elevating effect on the collective unconscious of humanity is immeasurable. Millions have learned to use their minds at a deeper and more effective level, even in their sleep!

With the Silva Method, you will learn how to:

Improve your health – mental and physical; improve your memory; unlock huge resources of the mind to master the ability to 'see' what you desire . . . then make it happen; increase your productivity; reach new goals; lead a happier, more fulfilling life; learn more quickly; overcome tension, bad habits and emotional insecurity; develop and control your will-power, and function at an inner conscious level for enhanced intuition, creativity, problem-solving ability and much more!

0 586 04850 2

The Successful Self
Freeing our Hidden Inner Strengths

Dorothy Rowe

Is it possible to be truly successful as a person? Or must we, as most of us do, continue to live our lives feeling in some way trapped and oppressed, frustrated, irritable, haunted by worries and regrets, creating misery for ourselves and others?

In *The Successful Self* leading psychologist Dorothy Rowe, author of *Beyond Fear*, shows us how to live more comfortably and creatively within ourselves by achieving a fuller understanding of how we experience our existence and how we perceive the threat of its annihilation.

She demonstrates how to develop the social and personal skills we lack, retaining the uniqueness of our individuality while becoming an integral part of the life around us and learning how to value and accept ourselves.

With characteristic originality, clarity and unfailing wisdom, Dorothy Rowe enables us to revolutionise our own lives and the lives of others in the process of becoming a Successful Self.

'Dorothy Rowe stands out amongst psychologists for her clear insight into human experience: her writing is refreshingly free from the dubious theoretical constructs and jargon ideas which plague this subject.'
Oliver Gillie, *Independent*

'A very brightly written book that intriguingly makes you question something most of us discuss: do we really like ourselves? Then ı goes on to help us do so.'
Mavis Nicholson

ISBN 0 00 637342 9

Learning to Lead

Developing Your Organization and Yourself

Bob Garratt

`His honesty, energy and intelligence shine through this book. Specifically aimed at top management, Garratt's intuitive judgement of directorial dilemmas and weaknesses is convincing'
Leadership and Organizational Development Journal

Learning is central to the survival and growth of all organizations. This unique book is the first to apply the theory that the key to company development is that leaders should be `direction givers' rather than mere `problem solvers'. *Learning to Lead*, which complements Garratt's previous book, *The Learning Organization*, explains thoroughly the directors' role in training and developing both themselves and their staff for increased efficiency, corporate self-esteem and market awareness, and goes on to examine the benefits of creating a learning organization and a learning climate.

`A much needed review with many novel insights into the design of 21st-century organizations'
MIKE BETT, Deputy Chairman, British Telecom

`Bob Garratt has addressed one of the key issues of our times, pulled it all together, and enriched it with his own perceptions'
PROFESSOR CHARLES HANDY,

ISBN 0 00 637722 X